THE
HOUSE
that
SERVICE
BUILT

The House that Service Built

Nancy Bandy

A Service of

NAHB

BuilderBooks.com™
National Association of Home Builders
1201 15th Street, NW
Washington, DC 20005-2800
(800) 223-2665
www.builderbooks.com

The House that Service Built
Nancy Bandy

Theresa Minch	Executive Editor
Jenny Stewart	Assistant Editor
Sharon Hamm	Copyeditor
E Design Communications	Cover Designer

BuilderBooks at the National Association of Home Builders

THERESA MINCH	Executive Editor
DORIS M. TENNYSON	Senior Acquisitions Editor
JESSICA POPPE	Assistant Editor
JENNY STEWART	Assistant Editor
BRENDA ANDERSON	Director of Fulfillment
GILL WALKER	Marketing Manager
JACQUELINE BARNES	Marketing Manager
GERALD HOWARD	NAHB Executive Vice President and CEO
MARK PURSELL	Executive Vice President Marketing & Sales
GREG FRENCH	Staff Vice President, Publications and Affinity Programs

ISBN 0-86718-559-7

© 2004 by BuilderBooks™
of the National Association of Home Builders
of the United States of America

Printed in the United States of America

Library of Congress
Cataloging in Publication Division
101 Independence Ave., S.E.
Washington, D.C. 20540-4320

Library of Congress Cataloging-in-Publication Data
Bandy, Nancy, 1950-
  The house that service built / Nancy Bandy.
    p. cm.
  ISBN 0-86718-559-7
  1. Construction industry—Customer services. I. Title.
  HD9715.A2B343 2004
  690'.068'8—dc22
                              2003020693

Disclaimer
This publication is designed to provide accurate and authoritative information in regard to the subject matter covered. It is sold with the understanding that the publisher is not engaged in rendering legal, accounting, or other professional service. If legal advice or other expert assistance is required, the services of a competent professional person should be sought.
                    —From a Declaration of Principles jointly adopted by a Committee of the American Bar Association
                    and a Committee of Publishers and Associations.

For further information, please contact:
BuilderBooks™
National Association of Home Builders
1201 15th Street, NW
Washington, DC 20005-2800
(800) 223-2665
Check us out online at: www.builderbooks.com

12/03 E Design Communications/Circle/[Printer]   2000

About the Author

Nancy Bandy is Managing Director of TRAINSITIONS Consulting Group LLC, a consulting firm that helps organizations use training initiatives to raise productivity and effectively adapt to the challenges of rapidly changing business environments. Nancy has more than 20 years of experience in corporate training, sales, and education, including management and executive positions with Coldwell Banker Corporation, Koll Management Services (now CB Richard Ellis), and Strategic HR Services, where she headed the global training division. Nancy's career has included corporate training and management development engagements with leading companies in a wide range of industries, giving her a unique perspective on solutions to the kinds of problems that companies are currently facing.

Nancy is a frequent public speaker at real estate industry events. She conducts regular workshops and training programs in the areas of consultative selling, management and instructor development, customer service, performance management, change management strategies, entrepreneurship, and executive leadership. Nancy is active in community affairs and presently serves on the Board of Directors of Pretend City®, a non-profit experiential learning museum for children.

Born in Belvidere, Illinois, Nancy holds a Bachelor of Science degree in Business Education & Administration from Northern Illinois University, with a Master's degree in Management from Webster University. She currently resides with her husband in Southern California.

Acknowledgments

In reflecting on how *The House that Service Built* finally came into existence, I have concluded that the defining forces which helped to take it from idea to reality fell into two key areas. For the actual content, the primary ideas and concepts presented within the pages of the book draw on both my education and years of experience in corporate training and management development. This experience has given me the opportunity to interact with successful companies and influential people across a broad swath of businesses, all the while acquiring useful perspectives from each contact.

My work in real estate and the building services industry has been especially relevant to the book, and for contributions here, I would like to single out and thank Barbara Dolim and Don Batz of the Mechanical Service Contractors of America, Chris Saunders of Pacific FM, and Bruce Shymanski of Service Excellence Corps for their continued support. Bob Mirman, CEO of Eliant, was especially helpful and is appreciated for sharing insights from the years of research his company has compiled on the home building industry and homebuyer preferences. The knowledge about homebuyer attitudes he has acquired since the start of his original company, National Survey Systems, would fill volumes.

My education formed the strong foundation on which these experiences could build. To all of my teachers throughout the years, thank you for showing me that learning is a lifelong process and for helping me establish early on a habitual quest for learning that has served me well in my career.

When it comes to motivation, the information acquired would never have made it between the pages of this book if not for the second key area, my all-important support group. These people provided the encouragement, prodding, and substantial contributions needed to actually convert my random and often incoherent ideas into what I hope you will find is an enjoyable and useful reference.

First and foremost, to my husband, who is both my partner as well as my closest friend in business and in life, I am eternally grateful. Without your constant support and highly honed editing talents, I'm sure this book would never have been completed.

To Theresa Minch, Executive Editor at Builder Books, thank you for your vision and help in making this book a reality. Thanks also to Jennifer Stewart for her watchful editing eye and guidance in keeping me on a practical timetable.

To John Telford at Webster University, thank you for forcing me through the invaluable exercise of creating a life plan that first included this book as one of its goals and turned out to be much more valuable than the grade received.

To Jack and Carol Hull, supporters as well as role models and long time good friends, thank you for your contributions and continued encouragement.

And finally, to my parents, Conrad and Aurelia Michel, thank you for instilling those values that led me to want to accomplish something more in life, as well as for providing the greatest support group of all, my sisters, Marie Garver, Linda Kelley and Diana Smith.

Contents

Figure List

Introduction

With all the theatrics of an award-winning actress, I pleaded with my husband. "Are you sure there's no way you can do this today?" He stared blankly at me with his outstretched body propped limply across the couch, one leg fully extended, the other bent and supported by a small mound of pillows. An ice-filled plastic bag rested on his knee, covering the mountain of bandages that had been applied after his surgery only two days earlier. He obviously wasn't going anywhere soon. Unquestionably, my request appeared selfish, insensitive, and even ridiculous, considering my husband's unfortunate condition.

I am normally considerate and sensitive to others' feelings—what could have driven me to this act of cruel desperation? I realized there was no way out; this time was my turn to face the car dealership's service department for the regular maintenance appointment. In my mind, this was an encounter to be avoided at all costs, one sure to make any nightmare pale in comparison.

Why would the thought of taking my automobile in to the dealer's "service" department send me into such fits of emotional irrationality? The answer is simple. Past experiences with the department's version of customer service had been anything but positive, involving rude and condescending service managers, time-wasting delays, broken commitments, and last-minute-repair-cost surprises that seemed to take advantage of my lack of automotive knowledge. My conditioning told me this time would be no different. I was certain that my already-limited time would be unnecessarily wasted, and in the end I would pay a premium price for the service abuse I expected as part of the process. And conversations with friends and business contacts had told me I was not alone in my experiences.

I don't mean to imply with my story that auto dealers have a monopoly on bad service. On a recent coast-to-coast trip, I counted 19 service failures from a variety of companies between my airport check-in and arrival at my hotel—and all this from a routine trip with a nonstop flight. In my travels around the country, I observe countless examples of poor customer service coming from leading corporations and smaller businesses alike. This reality is particularly distressing because these examples are from companies whose primary business is in what is referred to as the "service" industry. If that industry has problems with customer service, what must service be like from those companies in manufacturing or other non-service industries for which service is only a distant second to their primary role of producing actual products? As anyone who has tried to reach a real person at the end of a manufacturer's Help line, or who has attempted to get warranty repair for a newly purchased product can attest, the situation in the non-service sector is not encouraging, either.

When we as customers make the decision to buy a product or service, part of our purchase decision is based on the expectation that a reasonable level of customer service will accompany that purchase, to ensure quality and resolve any problems we might incur. Whether determined by actual written contract, or implied by advertising slogans to "stand behind the product," this "pact" is established in our minds as customers when we purchase the product, and a variety of consumer-protection laws and regulations often reinforce it.

When we consider the importance of service, how is it that so many companies have arrived at a point at which service no longer means helping customers but more often equates with neglecting, or even taking advantage, of them? Why have we allowed an environment to develop that drives once-loyal customers to competitors because of their frustration with our consistently poor customer service, which makes addressing even minor, easily corrected problems an unpleasant chore? This service breakdown causes otherwise successful companies to lose out against more responsive competitors and results in countless millions of dollars in lost business, needless expense, and costly litigation.

My firm belief is that most companies start out with good intentions to support their customers. Companies that have combined good products with strong customer-service capabilities establish legendary reputations and fantastically loyal customers who continue to buy from and promote those companies to friends, relatives, and business contacts. What company wouldn't want to be known for treating its customers so well that it enjoys the envious position from which a loyal customer base continues to grow without effort and is virtually resistant to competition?

Although it seems that good customer service should be second nature to any successful business, that reality is clearly not the case these days. Companies find that developing a reputation for good customer service does not happen overnight, because customer service goes much beyond just telling employees the customer is always right, or that they should be courteous and smile at customers who walk through the door. Companies go wrong in their pursuit of the customer service mission when they treat customer service as an afterthought or just another necessary expense of doing business. Customers are the most important consideration for any organization, and customer-service programs must be given this same level of priority. The decision to make customer service a key business strategy requires as much thought as any other important strategic decision the company might make, and this decision can have the same kind of impact on the bottom line.

To be successful, an organization needs to embrace customer service as a key part of its corporate culture. Once a company, division, or department is so committed, it can then develop appropriate customer-service initiatives to smoothly integrate this customer-service culture and associated policies into the overall business operations.

This book is designed to help organizations build their own unique customer-service cultures, using a systematic analysis and planning process to guide managers toward fully understanding customer expectations and how to best satisfy those needs. Although the techniques presented can apply to organizations of any size in virtually any industry, this book is written with a particular focus on the homebuilding industry and its particular customer, staffing, and market characteristics that affect the requirements for customer service. Like car dealerships and airlines, home builders are not immune to their share of service criticism, but the nature of this industry makes customer service even more critical to the home builder's success than might be true of other industry groups.

The book follows a logical sequence that takes the reader through the various steps needed to create an effective service culture. Chapter 1 first makes the financial case for good customer service by establishing the idea that service, although never quite free, should provide positive and measurable returns on investment, just like any other investment the company may choose to make. Once an organization makes the commitment to move forward, the specific steps outlined in chapters 2 through 8 create a roadmap for developing those goals, policies, and processes that form the service culture. The wrap-up for each chapter includes implications and recommendations that summarize how the concepts discussed can be applied to the home builder's market. At the end of each chapter are Action Plan Activities and thought-provoking questions, to reinforce the concepts presented in the context of the reader's own organization. For greatest benefit from the material, readers should complete each set of activities and questions before they move on to the next chapter.

Building a service strategy is much like building a home—you cannot put up the walls until the frame is built, and the frame cannot go up until the foundation is in place. *The House that Service Built* is your blueprint, and the individual chapters explore and explain each stage of development. The Action Plan Activities put the finishing touches on a chapter's topic, and they can be used as the basis for discussion and implementation at staff meetings and off-site retreats, as performance-measurement criteria for department heads and business line leaders, or as a personal development plan for individual readers. The end result of diligently following the steps outlined in each chapter will be a strategic plan for taking your organization to a higher level of service. This plan can transform your company into one of those legendary and successful industry leaders that your customers highly appreciate and your competitors greatly envy.

Does Service
Make Cents?

Is Good Service Good for Your Company?

A small group of people gathered in the hotel lobby for the nightly networking and idea exchange. Judging by the animated conversation, the conference these individuals were attending seemed to be a success. As they sipped drinks and munched on the assorted snacks hotel servers discreetly placed in front of them, one out-of-towner asked a question clearly designed to steer the discussion away from a rehash of the day's seminars, exhibits, and receptions. Already suspecting everyone's reaction, he took a deep breath, and with all the seriousness of a guard at Buckingham Palace asked this question: "Is good service a good thing for your companies?" Interspersed among chortles and laughter were such responses as "Of course!" "Are you kidding?" and "You aren't serious, are you?"

The question may seem simplistic, with an obvious answer, but carefully examined from a financial perspective, it may not be so absurd.

Is good customer service good business? Most business people and consumers alike would answer that question with a resounding Yes. But if you ask both groups to explain what good customer service means, you might be surprised to find little agreement on the answer. What does "good" customer service really mean, and, more importantly, what does it mean for the company's bottom line? We will attempt to answer these questions in the following pages. Before we do that, however, we will set the stage by reviewing historical developments that have led to the current view of customer service.

The Evolution of Customer Service

We can track the foundation of customer service back to some early consumer activism that led to new laws and agencies tasked with enforcing those laws to benefit the consumer. The Sherman Antitrust Act of 1890, along with its primary enforcement agency, the Federal Trade Commission, founded in 1914, were designed to provide consumers with fair choices among competitive manufacturers. The Pure Food and Drug Act was passed in 1906, and its companion Food and Drug Administration was founded, to ensure purity of foods and drugs for consumers. In the private sector, the formation of the Consumers Union in 1936, with the launch of its sister publication, *Consumer Reports,* reflected a growing consumer interest in better information on which to base product purchase decisions.

The advent of the modern consumer movement, starting with the publication in 1965 of Ralph Nader's book, *Unsafe at Any Speed,* energized interest in customer service as an important business function. This book chronicled how manufacturers endangered drivers by ignoring serious design flaws in their automobiles. Since that time, Nader's efforts in helping to create a number of consumer-activist organizations, and a continual stream of consumer-rights legislation, have been responsible for completely reshaping the relationship between manufacturers and their customers.

Even before Nader's pronouncements, the customer-service movement's two most dominant forces were already starting to take root. As early as 1956, the business dynamic was beginning to shift. For the first time in American history, white-collar workers outnumbered blue-collar workers. Rather than producing goods, Americans were instead starting to deliver services, with greater emphasis on customer interaction. A second major event occurred one year later, with the Russians sending the first satellite, Sputnik, into space. At the time, this event was viewed as the beginning of the space race. In retrospect, however, Sputnik's launch may have been much more significant as the birth of global communications.[1]

Twenty years later, the economy was starting a serious transformation from an industrial-based to an information-based society. This revolution further accelerated the trend toward services jobs, even while the manufacturing sector continued its decline. In 1982, the landmark book *In Search of Excellence* became a reference standard in executive boardrooms and college business curriculums because it captured the best practices of well-run companies in America. One consistent thread throughout these well-run companies was their attention to their customers and their customers' needs.[2] This focus firmly established the importance of customer service for business success in the minds of current and future corporate leaders. The other publication that received widespread attention in 1985 was *Service America!,* a book by Karl Albrecht and Ron Zemke, which showed a company how to turn its culture into a customer-driven and service-oriented one. In 1989, the authors followed their earlier work with *The Service Edge,* which took an in-depth look inside some of the companies that successfully used service as a key differentiator in their industries.

The 1990s completed the transition from the industrial era to the information age. Customer service has moved from the arena of forced consumer regulation to the point at which most companies recognize it is a competitive advantage. Even though the regulatory environment still exists, companies have fully embraced customer service as a business strategy that is a critical part of their business success.

Since the late 1980s, literally hundreds of books have been written about the value of customer service for successful businesses. Today, buzzwords, slogans, and corporate policies suggesting the importance of customer service abound. These indicators reflect the countless hours businesses have spent in corporate planning sessions and training programs

Customer Care refers to the process of understanding, communicating with, and supporting the needs of an organization's customers.

to get employees to meet the growing needs of a demanding public. This emphasis on customer service has been more than a token effort. Companies devote a considerable portion of their operating budgets to a variety of customer-service activities. Dataquest, Inc. has reported that companies on average spent more than $1 million per year to launch major customer-relationship management initiatives, with that number continuing to grow.[3] The financial reports of service-oriented companies indicate that customer-support budgets can be as high as 16 percent of the total operating budget.[4] Purdue Research Foundation found that budget allocations for companies with formal call centers included such items as salaries, computer hardware and software, recruiting, training, and even real estate.[5]

CUSTOMER RELATIONSHIP BUDGET ITEMS	
Salary and Benefits	58.13%
Recruiting, Screening, Training	4.96%
Telecommunications Network Provider	5.48%
Computer Software	3.97%
Telecommunications Equipment	4.45%
Real Estate	4.55%
Outsourced Calls	1.9%

The most recent references to customer service as a key part of *Customer Care* or *Customer Relationship Management (CRM)* programs suggest a higher level of importance and an enterprise-wide perspective that makes providing customer service and attending to customer needs a critical function within any successful organization. Although it is true that everyone in an organization should be

Figure 1-1 Evolution of Customer Service

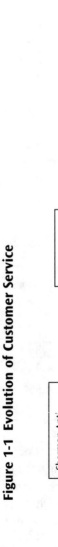
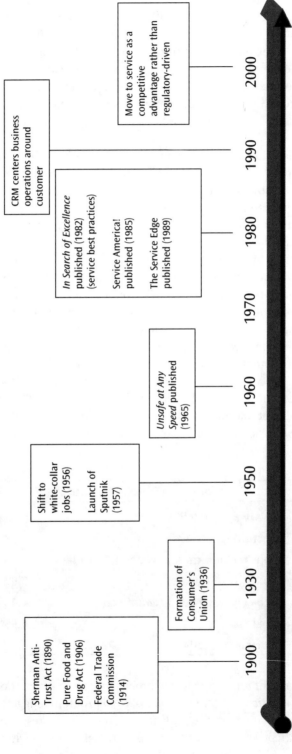

Sherman Anti-Trust Act (1890)

Pure Food and Drug Act (1906)

Federal Trade Commission (1914)

Formation of Consumer's Union (1936)

Shift to white-collar jobs (1956)

Launch of Sputnik (1957)

Unsafe at Any Speed published (1965)

In Search of Excellence published (1982) (service best practices)

Service America! published (1985)

The Service Edge published (1989)

CRM centers business operations around customer

Move to service as a competitive advantage rather than regulatory-driven

1900   1930   1950   1960   1970   1980   1990   2000

responsive to customer needs, this perspective doesn't change the fact that customer service has been in the past, and remains today, primarily a person-to-person activity. Those individuals most directly affected by the customer-service benefits a business provides tend to value those benefits, whether the individuals are acting on their own or as representatives of their organizations.

Customer Care includes the customer-service function, but where traditional customer service has been primarily reactive after problems occur, the Customer Care function aims to be proactive in communicating with and managing information about customers to better understand and anticipate their needs before problems arise.

Customer Relationship Management (CRM) is an industry term for methodologies, technology, and capabilities that help an organization manage customer relationships in an organized and efficient manner.

Although CRM is often attributed to software applications that may form the core of a CRM initiative, its objective is to provide workers with the information and processes necessary to know their customers, understand their needs, and communicate effectively with, and build stronger relationships between, the company, its customer base, and its service partners.

For all their good intentions to establish responsive customer-service capabilities, most companies today still can't tell you exactly what "good" customer service is, or how effective they are in providing it to satisfy their customers' needs. It should not be surprising, therefore, to find that companies' efforts to provide good customer service often fall short of their intended objectives.

Study after study shows that, for the most part, consumers don't feel they receive very good levels of customer service by those providers they deal with. The latest figures from the American Consumer Satisfaction Index (ACSI), a nationwide satisfaction indicator developed by the University of Michigan Business School, shows that, with few exceptions, customer satisfaction has either decreased or remained relatively stagnant in almost every area of business since the index was started in 1994.[6] This national index is compiled by measuring customer satisfaction within 38 different industries using a 100-point scale.

Clearly, these findings suggest that the substantial investment and effort that most companies devote to customer-service programs have not been very effective in delivering satisfactory results to their customers. For the committed leader, this is a disturbing finding that merits immediate attention to correct. Instead of continuing to do things the way they have been done in the past, companies must now look in a completely new way at customer service and the processes they use to provide it to their customers.

In the following pages, we will attempt to better define what good customer service really means, and what its true value is to service providers and the customers they are serving. From this starting point, we will look at how companies can develop strategies to most effectively provide service that meets the real needs of their customers, while contributing to the overall success of the business.

Figure 1-2 Customer Satisfaction Statistics

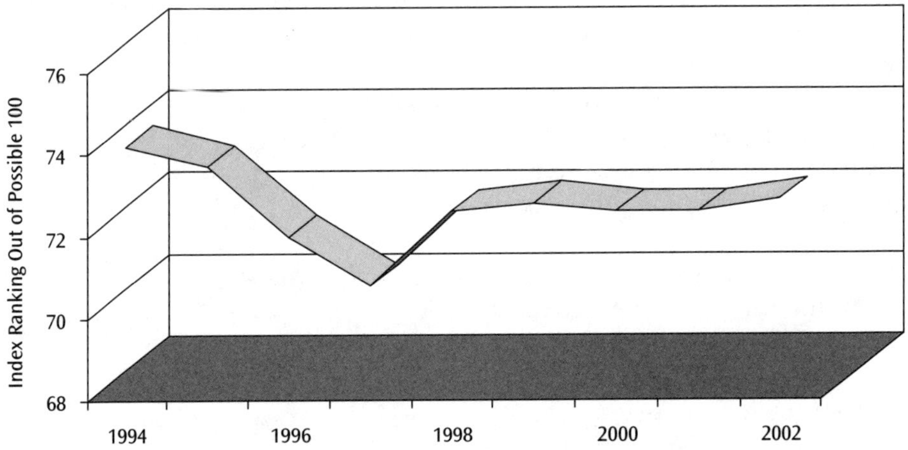

Source: American Customer Satisfaction Index, National Quarterly Scores, 1994–2002
http://www.theacsi.org

Customer Service, Exposed

Most of us would probably agree that we can distinguish between good and bad service after we have experienced the two extremes, but we would probably be hard pressed to define exactly what characterizes those extremes of service quality and the various levels in between. Why is categorizing customer service so difficult? There are a number of reasons for this inherent challenge in the fundamental character of the service process.

Unlike a manufactured product that has specific features and dimensions, service is an intangible that cannot be easily categorized. The many variables involved in meeting customer needs change from one situation to the next, which makes the service needs contingent upon the product, the circumstances, and the environment in which service is provided. The service delivery process cannot be easily separated from the people delivering, and the customers receiving, the service. The varying expectations of the individuals involved can affect the outcome of the delivery. Good service is in the eye of the beholder and is measured by each individual's personal expectations.

Good service is in the eye of the beholder and is measured by each individual's personal expectations.

Customer Service—the Consumer's View

Customer service for the consumer generally means "actions that satisfy individual customer needs concerning a product before, during, and after the product purchase." Customer needs can refer to almost anything involving or related to the product. Need categories typically include the following:

■ Product information
■ Advice

GOOD VERSUS BAD CUSTOMER SERVICE	
Good Customer Service	**Bad Customer Service**
Providing easy accessibility to service provider, including immediate option for talking to a live person.	Offering multiple menu selections when telephone is answered by automated attendant, with no option for talking to a live person.
Proactively keeping customers informed of work status.	Communicating work status only when customer inquires about it.
Performing the service right the first time.	Performing service haphazardly, requiring customers to make repeated requests.
Honoring promises and commitments.	Misrepresenting the product or service to make a sale.
Willingly providing service in a timely and prompt manner.	Making it difficult for customers to get appointments for service.
Ensuring the neat, professional appearance of service provider's uniforms, tools, and equipment.	Presenting slovenly and unkempt appearance of service provider's uniforms, tools, and equipment.

- Education prior to the sale
- Selection
- Option configuration
- Order entry
- Purchase assistance during the sale
- Repair or problem resolution
- Maintenance
- Training
- Application assistance after the sale
- Product information

Customer Service—the Provider View

Do product providers view customer service in the same way? We would expect customers and providers alike to embrace the basic concept of satisfying user needs, and this is true in principle. In today's environment, the manufacturer has an ethical, competitive, and legal obligation to provide service to the customer in return for the customer's commitment to purchase the product. The perspective the service provider takes in actually accomplishing this, however, is necessarily a little different from that of the customer.

The manufacturer's view is that service is a necessary complement to selling the product. When done well, service leads to satisfied customers, reduced complaints, and positive corporate image, resulting in increased sales and profits. Because almost all companies are in business for the purpose of producing a profit, a primary reason and justification for providing customer service is to enhance profits by expanding total sales and reducing the costs of achieving those sales. To do otherwise might mean that a company would not be able to continue to support its customers, or even survive in that business for the long run.

Customer service for the manufacturer or service provider can then be defined as "the mix of activities undertaken to satisfy customer needs concerning the product before, during, and after the product sale and that provide an acceptable return on investment (ROI)."

The common ground between the user's and the provider's viewpoint is satisfaction of customer needs, and there is little argument that this should be the objective for any customer-service program. The provider's additional focus on ROI is not necessarily contradictory to that objective. The consumer in some fashion will make a decision about price versus benefits for any product purchase, and the level of service expected is one of those benefits that factors into the price equation. The manufacturer providing the service must also make decisions about what level of resources and capital is appropriate to devote to the customer-service function, as one aspect of the price-versus-profit consideration. Because most companies have a range of investment opportunities for their capital and resources, they must be able to justify their investment in customer service on the basis of the return expected; this justification should also be a primary consideration in defining any customer-service strategy.

If the company is to maximize return from an investment in customer service, it must go well beyond meeting basic customer needs, to the point of exceeding customer expectations. A customer-service program that does this will provide the greatest benefits to the company and its customers alike. Service that exceeds expectations and leaves customers highly satisfied with the experience and the product is what can be properly called "good" customer service.

Service that exceeds expectations and leaves customers highly satisfied with the experience and the product is what can be properly called "good" customer service.

Factors That Influence How Customer Service Is Perceived and Valued

A number of factors have an impact on how customer service will affect customers' expectations, their level of satisfaction, and the effective value of any service they receive. Recognizing these underlying factors is important to understanding how to achieve the objective of delivering good customer service.

Relationship between Product Quality and Customer Service

Customer service can have a dramatic effect on customers' perceptions of product quality and their overall satisfaction with the product. When customers experience product quality problems, good customer-service practices can help to quickly restore or even raise customer-satisfaction levels above what they would have been if no problems had occurred. The nature of this relationship between quality, service, and satisfaction is to a great extent dependent on the characteristics of the product itself.

Customers can be expected to value service differently, depending on what the product is and does. For basic, standardized products, customer service may be a less important part of the initial selection and purchase decision, because consumers do not need a lot of assistance in choosing the product, and they do not expect much to go wrong once the product is in their hands. The service expectation may not extend much beyond the delivery process itself, but the customer service provided can still influence the overall value to customers by raising the perception of quality for the product. In these instances, the function of service is primarily to reinforce the quality image of the manufacturer and, by inference, the branded product.

Providing a level of service for a product that might otherwise be indistinguishable from other similar products helps to differentiate that product from the others. This perceived higher value can give the product an advantage over competitors' products and justify higher pricing than possible without the service component. Companies routinely take advantage of this service-quality relationship to price their products differently or to charge extra for the product with different levels of warranty or service/support.

For more complex products, customer service can also be associated with higher product quality, but it also takes on an entirely different role. With more sophisticated products, the customer service becomes much more an integral component of the product itself, and an important part of the overall purchase decision. (Large office copiers, medical diagnostic equipment, or luxury automobiles are examples of these types of products.) The role of customer service in these situations is more important to ensure performance of the complex product, and it serves to reduce decision and ownership risk for the purchaser. A high level of service means that, no matter what, customers have the assurance they will receive the benefits they expected when they purchased the product. Without an adequate customer-service component to convince customers that risk in purchasing the product is minimized, the sale may become much more difficult and costly, with significant price or other concessions necessary to overcome this obstacle.

Relationship between Time and Customer Satisfaction

For anyone who has had to wait in an incredibly long line at a government "service" agency, who has been put on hold with toll charges running when he or she was trying to get information from a so-called Help desk, or who has had to wait an hour beyond the designated appointment time in the doctor's office for a "scheduled" appointment that was set up three months in advance, it should come as no surprise that the time element is an important part of the customer's satisfaction with services provided. Several different time categories can have important impacts on customer satisfaction.

Response Time

Most fundamental of the time relationships is the time required for the customer to actually reach someone who can either immediately address the customer's issue or provide a reliable commitment for the service needed to do so.

The expectation about what an appropriate response time should be will vary with the product and situation. Shortest possible response may almost always seem preferable, but the resource costs required to provide service such as 24/7-staffed Help lines or maintenance capabilities may be unacceptably high. And, in many cases, providing immediate resolution of problems may not be necessary to achieve high customer-satisfaction levels. As long as time-critical situations can be prioritized and responded to quickly, while reliable commitments are provided for resolving other non-critical problems, a longer resolution time may be acceptable. For the provider, such assurance means that a resource plan and budget are needed that can provide an optimal and appropriate response time for the situation. A two-week response time may be perfectly acceptable when the issue is a general information request or a repair of peeling paint, but a two-hour response time may be considered too long when the problem is a water or gas leak.

Regardless of the time required to actually deliver the service, the response time for the initial contact and actual commitment to resolve should be kept as short as possible. Customers often will be much more tolerant of longer resolution time and even unanticipated delays in resolving problems if they feel they are being given appropriate attention with personal contact, commitment, and status updates. The level of frustration and dissatisfaction escalates rapidly when the customer cannot quickly get in contact with the service provider.

Latency

Another measure of time that affects customer expectations for service after the sale is *latency*. Latency refers to the dormant period between the initial purchase of the product and the time that the service request is made. In most cases, the customer has expectations prior to the purchase of receiving a "near-perfect" product with no problems that would require service. (Why would a customer have purchased a product with known problems?) The expectation for fast response and resolution in this instance is high. Long after the purchase, and perhaps near the end of the product's usable life, the expectations are much lower, and customer satisfaction may be achieved with a much different level of customer service.

A warranty period can distort the latency relationship between time and customer satisfaction. Whereas customer expectations during the life of the product may gradually decline as time passes from the original purchase date, the effect of the warranty is to maintain customer expectations at a level close to what they might have been at initial purchase. The warranty period itself may be determined more by competitive forces, but it becomes an important consideration in setting service resource levels adequate to support the customer expectations that the warranty creates.

Post-Purchase Dissonance and the Time Element

The aspect of buying behavior referred to as *post-purchase dissonance,*[7] or *buyer's remorse,* as it is more commonly referred to by real-estate agents, makes the period immediately following the purchase decision one of special importance in terms of providing service. In simple terms, post-purchase dissonance refers to the idea that any doubts the customer had before the purchase tend to be amplified after the purchase commitment has been made. Because this reaction is mostly emotional, the customer may be much more highly sensitive to any service failures or delayed responses during this time. The service experience is a way to resolve issues, lower anxiety, and reduce the potential impact of post-purchase dissonance during this sensitive period when otherwise minor issues may escalate to major problem status as a result of the purchaser's heightened sensitivity.

The service program should be designed to recognize this particular effect and give high priority to a customer's service needs immediately following the purchase decision, and until such time as the post-purchase anxiety has dissipated. Many manufacturers address this important effect with special programs such as "no-questions asked" returns, or immediate product replacement, both designed to minimize the post-purchase dissonance effect.

How Customer Satisfaction Affects the Bottom Line

In attempts to convey the message that customer service is a high priority in their business, companies emphasize service campaigns that include highly visible

Figure 1-3 Influence of Time on Customer Service Expectations

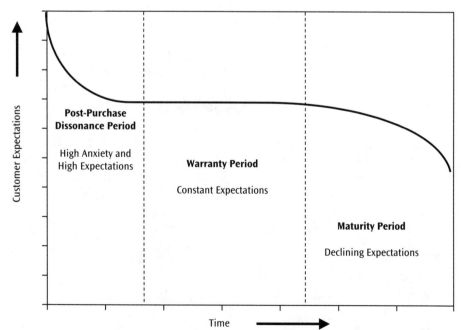

buttons, posters, and materials declaring their devotion to the customer. After they have poured a substantial amount of money into these initiatives, however, these companies often are disappointed with the results.

Although customers are often happier and more satisfied with their service interactions than they were before, this satisfaction doesn't always translate into a measurable increase in company sales and profits. Without visible results, for a company to justify the resources and investment needed to provide a high level of service in the future is difficult. The reason for this failing is that most companies don't fully understand how their customers value service, or how good customer service can actually contribute financially to the company's sales and profits.

Most companies provide service as an afterthought to the product sale. They consider service as an overhead expense that is a necessary part of doing business, required more to avoid or correct for the rare product-quality or delivery failure than as something that can actively contribute to increased revenue and profits. For companies with this view, the entire goal usually becomes one of holding customer-service expenses to the minimum needed to keep customer complaints at tolerable levels.

This perspective on customer service is unfortunate because it ignores the fundamental role of customer service in support of the product sale. When they view customer service as an integral requirement for the product sale, companies can set an actual value on the customer-service component and even charge additionally for it, in which case customer service can become a separately measurable profit-and-loss item. Almost always, the customer-service experience represents a unique opportunity after the initial sale for the company to interact with customers and enhance their positive impressions of the company and its products. This positive contact also offers the opportunity to sell additional or complementary products with minimal added effort. Most sales people actively look for ways to get more "face" time with their customers, in situations in which they can reinforce the company's image and increase potential for repeat or complementary product sales.

Almost always, the customer-service experience represents a unique opportunity after the initial sale for the company to interact with customers and enhance their positive impressions of the company and its products.

Viewed in this light, service has the potential to actually contribute significantly to the company's bottom line, providing an attractive return on investment that can rival other opportunities that the company might have for investment of available capital and resources.

KEY ROLES CUSTOMER SERVICE PLAYS

- Raises the perception of product quality.
- Lowers the acquisition risk for the customer.
- Differentiates the product to allow for more effective sales against competition.
- Helps to avoid the need for discount pricing.

HERE IS A SUMMARY OF WAYS IN WHICH CUSTOMER SERVICE CAN MAKE A POSITIVE AND MEASURABLE CONTRIBUTION TO THE BOTTOM LINE:

- Develop repeat sales by building strong brand loyalty with existing customers so that they become customers for life. As a personal-relationship experience, customer service has the ability to build much stronger customer loyalty than is possible when the company relies solely on product benefits or quality alone. As every good salesperson will tell you, "People buy from people, not companies."

- Bring in additional referral business as the result of word-of-mouth evangelizing from highly satisfied customers. These testimonials build new business without the added expense of advertising, cold calling, or special promotions.

- Permit premium pricing over competitors who do not provide the same level of customer service.

- Allow for complementary product sales through the positive customer contact and exposure opportunity that is part of the customer-service experience.

- Provide an additional, separately priced service component that contributes incremental sales and profits to the basic product sale.

Research Backs the Relationship between Customer Service and Profits

TARP, a research and consulting firm established at Harvard University in 1971, has conducted extensive research on customer behaviors since the early 1970s. TARP's research confirms a direct correlation between customer loyalty and the service experience. The more highly satisfying the service experience is, the greater the loyalty, repeat sales, and referrals that result for the service provider. TARP has proposed a model for estimating the effect that positive customer service can have on a company's profits as a result of this repeat sale loyalty and increased referral rate. Using this model, Figure 1-4 shows the estimates of the additional profit for the typical homebuilder when satisfaction levels increase. In this figure, the TARP model indicates as much as 4.5 percent in additional profit just from the resulting increased retention and referrals when high satisfaction levels for customer service are achieved.[8]

University of Michigan research on satisfaction also suggests that companies with highly satisfied customers tend to show this customer satisfaction in their bottom lines and resulting stock-price valuations. In the U of M research, increases in customer satisfaction ratings correlated positively with increases in the stock price for those companies that were able to raise satisfaction levels, compared to stock prices of their lesser-ranked competitors.[9]

Customers develop loyalty and encourage additional business with companies from which they receive gratifying service experiences. Conversely, they don't return to, and don't recommend to others, products from companies

Figure 1-4 Profit Gain from Customer Service

$Profit Added

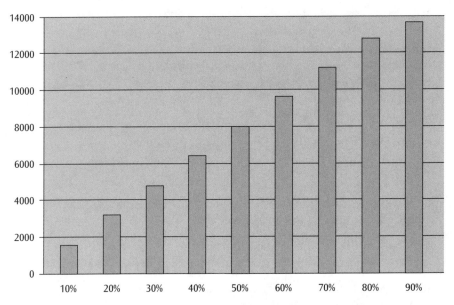

Percentage of Customers Highly Satisfied with Service

with which they have had unsatisfactory experiences or have had unmet needs as part of the product purchase. The influence of the service experience on the customer is such that it can sometimes become an even more important determinant of the product purchase decision than the basic features and quality of the product itself.

Quantifying Customer Service Satisfaction Levels

In developing a customer-service program with positive returns, it is important to measure the levels of quality and responsiveness required to satisfy customer-service needs for a specific product. For an appropriate performance and investment-return assessment, companies must be able to determine customer-satisfaction levels in relation to some desired result, and to monitor service provided to see that the resources and investment provided in support of the customer-service initiative are achieving these goals.

Although it is not always possible to categorize in advance precisely what actions comprise good and bad customer service for a given situation, it is possible to assess to what degree the customer was satisfied with the service provided. The level of customer satisfaction is a relative assessment of how well the provided service met customer expectations for the circumstances of the specific service incident.

- If the customer's expectations are met or exceeded, then the experience is viewed as positive or even exceptional.
- When the customer's expectations are not met, or only minimally met, customer perception of the service experience becomes neutral, neither significantly positive nor negative.
- When added frustrations, delays, unpleasant encounters, or unanticipated costs are part of a marginal service episode, the service experience may become highly negative or even confrontational.

Surveys using a satisfaction-ranking scale are a good way to assess the quality of the service experience for the customer. Following are typical survey classifications for rating satisfaction that fall into the classical 5-point or 10-point scale.

From the manufacturer's perspective, one extreme brings negative results in the form of complaints, word-of-mouth negative comments, or even negative press and publicity when issues become public knowledge. The other extreme results in positive referrals and publicity from "happy customer" comments and unsolicited testimonials. One extreme results in a hasty departure of the customer, never to be seen again; the other results in long-term loyalty with repeat purchases and new sales opportunities.

Figure 1-5 shows a typical survey-ranking method by which customers can rate their satisfaction with customer service. The classification names are arbitrary and can change from survey to survey. The meaning suggested by the ranking extremes, on a 5-, 10-, or any other category scale, are clear. Implications for rankings in these various categories—unacceptable, below expectations, satisfactory, above expectations, and exceptional—are discussed below.

Unacceptable. This satisfaction level is likely when a customer's needs that prompted the original request are not met, when additional problems are created as a result of the service provided, or when a difficult interaction with the service provider occurs during the delivery process.

Let's suppose new homeowners need warranty work done on their furnace after their recent move-in. Their expectations upon calling the trade contractor are that the furnace will be fixed as quickly as possible when the technician makes the service visit to their home. Imagine their frustration when the technician is late in arriving, is unable to fix the problem immediately, cannot give a commitment for when the work will be completed, and in the process of the visit tracks dirt onto their new carpeting. Not only was the furnace left in disrepair, but the customers experienced

Figure 1-5 Typical Satisfaction Survey Ratings

How would you rate the quality of service you received?				
Exceptional	Above Expectations	Satisfactory	Below Expectations	Unacceptable
☐	☐	☐	☐	☐

major inconveniences, and even damages, which showed lack of consideration for them and established a poor quality expectation.

Customers in this category are likely to form a highly negative opinion of the service supplier, which is also quickly associated with the product. At a minimum, such an experience leads to a strong decision not to repurchase, along with comments to others recommending against purchase of this supplier's products. In the worst case, recovery of damages from, or even legal action against, the supplier may result. Providing service that falls into this category is like spending money on advertising that says, "Buy our products, then go away," which is exactly what happens. This category is obviously not one into which any provider would choose to be ranked.

Below expectations. This satisfaction level is the likely result when customer needs are met, but when the overall service experience still falls short of what was expected or committed to.

Going back to our example of the furnace warranty work, the homeowners would have been left unhappy if the technician was able to fix the furnace, but he was several hours late in arriving, and he still left dirt on the carpeting.

Customers ranking in this category are not likely to recommend this supplier, and they probably will not be repeat purchasers in the future without some corrective action. However, even minor recovery actions by the manufacturer still may be able to maintain a positive customer view of the product, especially if the service episode is viewed as an isolated event not representing the normal standards of the provider.

Satisfactory. Service providers simply doing their jobs in an unremarkable way would probably elicit responses with this ranking. This rating represents an average or neutral satisfaction rating from customers.

Although the customer needs that initiated the request may have been met, little of note occurred in the process of the service delivery to raise the customer's perception of the product or the provider's company. The furnace is fixed, and the work area is left in the same condition as before the repair began.

On the surface, this may seem a desirable outcome. The reality is that this average experience for the customer should be considered a minimum performance level for the provider, because it means the provider has missed an excellent opportunity to enhance the customer's perception about the quality of the company and its products. The impression created in the customer's mind is that the company and its products are just "average." Instead of looking to the company for the next buying opportunity, the customer may instead shop competitors who appear to have higher-quality products and better customer service.

Above Expectations. When the customer's needs are fully met, with a prompt and efficiently orchestrated delivery, the customer develops a favorable impression of the product and the service provider, which results in increased loyalty and repeat purchases for the products. However, the impression is probably not sufficient to turn the customer into an active evangelist for the company and its products.

When the service provider arrives at the designated time and displays courtesy, consideration, and respect for the customer's property by scraping shoe bottoms before stepping on new flooring, these actions will no doubt please the customer. Additional points are earned if the problem is fixed in an efficient and courteous manner without any incident, leaving the customer with a positive impression of the service provider.

Exceptional. This rating results when the original service needs are met with unusual speed or efficiency, and when the delivery experience and interactions with the providers are well beyond what the customer expected.

Again, looking at the furnace-repair scenario, what would have happened if the service technician appeared at the customer's door as scheduled, but before he walked on the customer's brand new floor, he placed foot covers over his work shoes to prevent any outside dirt from getting tracked in? A further gesture that would enhance loyalty would be for the service representative to explain to the customers how they could use the setback feature on their thermostat to reduce heating costs in the future. These small gestures, which cost little or nothing and took minimal effort, would have so impressed the new homeowners that the service call would have created a memorable experience in their minds, and one worth telling other people about. Often, this type of small but considerate effort, which shows large concern for the customer, can be the deciding factor that moves a service event from the "average" to the "exceptional" category. Customers whose evaluations fall into this category tend to become highly valuable, unsolicited evangelists for the company and its products.

Relating Satisfaction Levels to Sales and Profits

How does quantifying satisfaction in these ways help companies start to understand the benefits they are providing to their customers, and the potential returns they can expect on their investment in customer service?

TARP's research found that a majority of the consuming public falls within the middle range for satisfaction levels, which means that these are individuals who have simply had "average or unremarkable" experiences.

This group of consumers represents both a danger and an opportunity for the service provider. The TARP data mean that a large number of consumers are "on the fence" and have only a neutral impression of the product or provider. If handled properly, these consumers can be moved into the higher satisfaction levels, where they are more likely to become repeat customers. If nothing is done, or this group is not serviced well, its members can as easily shift in the other direction, where they form a negative impression of the product and are inclined to search out other suppliers. By converting even a small percentage of the individuals in this group to a higher satisfaction level, a company can significantly increase its business by retaining these existing customers and by benefiting from the increased word-of-mouth referrals that such loyal customers will generate.

TARP research also indicates that the greatest benefits to an organization from its customer-service programs result when the programs go well beyond just satisfying the customer, to the point of substantially exceeding customer expectations.[10] Studies from Eliant (formerly known as National Survey Systems), a research firm specializing in the homebuilding industry, back up this hypothesis and refer to this state as "Legendary Service."[11] Highly satisfied customers are those who have been moved from indifference to a position of strong loyalty, from which they become enthusiastic supporters and evangelists for the company's products. These groups provide invaluable endorsements and word-of-mouth recommendations to a large number of potential customers. TARP statistics show that these high-satisfaction customers are 50 percent more likely to be repeat buyers and evangelists for the company's products than are those who are only marginally satisfied with the products or service.[12]

TARP statistics show that these high-satisfaction customers are 50 percent more likely to be repeat buyers and evangelists for the company's products than are those who are only marginally satisfied with the products or service.

> Customer service after the sale can be compared to treating an injury or illness. When an accurate and prompt diagnosis is made, followed by properly prescribed treatment, injuries are repaired, and ultimately the patient is stronger and happier than if nothing had been done. When the diagnosis is incorrect, and treatment is delayed or inadequate, a minor injury can become serious and potentially life threatening. When the injury is the need for customer service after the sale, incorrect diagnosis, or delayed or inadequate treatment, can cause irreparable harm to the relationship between the customer and the organization that the service provider represents.

How Customer Satisfaction Hurts the Bottom Line

Given the relative ease of diagnosing and fixing problems early by providing an exceptional level of customer service, one wonders why more companies don't commit to it. Trying to recover business lost from the departure of an irate and unhappy customer is much more expensive than the effort required to correct problems in the first place and keep that customer as a satisfied, repeat buyer of the product.

> TARP data estimates that, across a range of businesses, developing new customers ends up costing from 2 to 20 times as much as providing the good customer service necessary to keep current customers highly satisfied and loyal to the company and its products.[13]

By TARP's measures, most consumers fit into categories in which they find the service experience to be a neutral or negative influence on the impressions they form about the product or the service provider—impressions that will affect their future buying behavior.

When customers fall into these categories, what actions are they likely to take? A number of responses are possible, depending on how unhappy the customers are, what their original expectations for the product and service were, the circumstances under which problems occurred; and even the personal styles of the individual customers. All these factors can have a negative effect on the company's sales and profits. Marginally satisfied customers may fall into one of the categories shown in Figure 1-6.

Human responses can include both a *rational* and an *emotional* component, and the balance between the two is often determined by the intensity of the dissatisfaction that results from the service episode. Most people start with a logical perspective, with the emotional component taking on more and more importance as the level of frustration rises. Highly emotional negative responses can be especially difficult to deal with and are potentially most damaging to the organization.

Indifferent customers are those most likely to fall into the silent-majority category, in which they have had an "average" service episode. The service effort in this case is not noteworthy, and it neither contributes to nor detracts from the expectations for the product. From this view, the experience is somewhat negative because the laissez-faire attitude established almost invites the customer to look for something better at the next buying opportunity. Indifferent customers are usually in abundance, but they are hard to identify because they are unlikely to be very outspoken either positively or negatively.

Indirect complainers may have had their needs met, but they may have had other negative experiences as part of the service episode. Like the indifferent

Figure 1-6 Possible Actions of Indifferent or Dissatisfied Customers

Customer Category	Service Experience	Possible Customer Responses
Silent Majority	Basic needs were met, but service was otherwise unmemorable	No particular loyalty Comparison shopper in future Easily converted to competitor
Indirect Complainer	Needs may or may not have not been met Other negatives may have occurred that left the customer unhappy with the service	Not fully satisfied with service Will not complain to someone who could take action May comment to line staff Negative comments to others likely May shop competition at next purchase
Direct Complainer	Needs were unmet, and the service experience may have included major problems or negligence	Aggressive and formal complaints Multiple negative recommendations May complain to regulatory agencies Legal action possible Protests and boycotts in extreme cases

customers above, these customers are sometimes not visible to management because they don't openly express their concerns about the service when problems occur, or, if they do say something, it is usually a comment in passing to line staff, who may have had no direct involvement, or who have no responsibility for the service action.

For these two types of responses, the customer will not volunteer information to the service provider, so it becomes important to use proactive methods such as follow-up calls or surveys to discover and correct the causes of these attitudes as quickly as possible. In these cases, silence is not golden; rather, it can be a false security that masks underlying negative attitudes and inadequate customer service.

Silence is not golden; rather it can be a false security that masks underlying negative attitudes and inadequate customer service.

Direct complainers are those for whom the service experience was far enough off the desired objective that it elicits an active, more aggressive, and often emotional response. The manufacturer will probably know about these customers because they will be very vocal in expressing their dissatisfaction to the service provider and to others, as well.

Although *aggressive complaints* can often be unnerving to front-line staff who receive them, these complaints at least give the provider an opportunity to correct the service shortcomings. When the unhappy consumer doesn't say anything about the issues of concern, as with the first two categories, the service provider must take a very proactive approach to find out about problems and take corrective action.

Customers in the aggressive-complaints category will probably require significant and costly actions to overcome the negatives of the service experience. It may not be possible to recover them as future customers, but addressing their concerns is extremely important, to minimize the damage for the company in negative publicity and lost sales with other potential customers.

Personal styles also may suppress the normal actions that customers might take relative to their satisfaction levels. Everyone probably has personal experience with people who could be labeled *natural complainers.* This type of personality, depicted by complaints about some aspect of the service experience regardless of the relative quality of the service delivered, may be very demanding and especially difficult to satisfy.

At the other end of the spectrum, some people tend to be more passive in avoiding conflict situations and may be unlikely to complain regardless of their satisfaction level. The following sidebar shows why people don't take the time to actively voice their complaints about inferior service. These personality types can also create difficult problems for the provider because such customers may inadvertently mask problems that the provider would prefer to correct if it were made aware of them. The service provider can effectively address the issue of personal style in relation to satisfaction with pro-active follow-up that assesses a number of parameters about the service experience.

WHY CUSTOMERS DON'T COMPLAIN

Most companies want to know when their customers are not satisfied, so they can correct problems that make for unhappy customers. The natural assumption is that a low level of complaints implies few problems. The reality, various market research studies have shown, is that few customers actually complain about product or service-quality problems to someone who could take action. Why is it that customers don't complain?

- Most people don't like confrontation. Because of this, they may avoid raising issues with those who are directly providing a product or service. Unfortunately, these same people may repeatedly complain about the service later to other third parties in less confrontational situations.

- Complaining can be frustrating, with little expectation that it will help correct a problem that has already occurred. Why waste time complaining if it won't fix the problem?

- Complaining takes time and effort. To ensure that your complaint lands in the hands of someone empowered to make a difference, you have to dedicate time to researching the organizational structure, finding names and locations of the proper parties, and then composing your complaint in writing so that it is clearly understood by the reader. All that takes a lot of effort and time, resources which are already too scarce for today's busy consumers, especially if they feel their labors won't do them any good.

- It's easier to move to another product. Today's competitive environment provides many attractive alternatives when customers become unhappy with a product. It may be too late for this purchase, but it's easier to just keep quiet and make the decision to switch to another company next time, rather than complain to a supplier who doesn't seem to care as much about its customers.[14]

Financial Implications of Poor Quality Customer Service

Previously, we looked at ways that an investment in customer service can provide positive returns to the organization when the service delivered meets the needs of customers. When customer service fails to meet customer needs because of limited resources, inadequate training, or poor execution, the opposite situation unfortunately occurs, and there can be serious negative financial implications. Possible negative financial impacts from poor customer service include the following:

- Higher sales costs needed to identify and sell to new customers, replacing those who moved to competitors because of dissatisfaction with the current product and service
- Increased advertising and promotion costs needed to restore a corporate image badly damaged by negative publicity

- Costs to correct and compensate for damages resulting from low-quality service episodes
- Penalties and discovery costs associated with regulatory audits initiated by customer complaints
- Litigation defense and damages settlements to very dissatisfied (former) customers

Any or all of these outcomes can occur in those cases in which customer satisfaction falls into the average or lower satisfaction levels. Companies should consider these possible negatives as potential risks to be aware of when they are developing customer-service strategies. Because the financial downside from some of these factors can be extraordinarily high, the goal of every organization obviously should be to provide customer service at high performance levels that avoid these damaging losses to the organization.

Customer Service for the Home Builder

In this chapter, you have read about the general concepts and considerations that are important for any business wishing to provide good service for its customers. Needs of customers in different markets can vary dramatically, thus requiring different approaches to the design of the customer-service programs that serve those industries.

The homebuilding industry is unique in that it is providing highly complex and costly products for direct sale to the homeowner, who in most cases will be relatively unknowledgeable about the details of home construction and financing. A home "product" purchase is an intimidating experience for the average consumer. The typical home involves hundreds of different materials; a number of separate subsystems, such as electrical, plumbing, and air conditioning; and dozens of different contractors, permits, and inspections that involve hundreds of different employees. The home is probably the highest-cost and most-complex product the average consumer will ever purchase.

A number of important implications for the home builder can be drawn from these concepts for the development of an effective customer-service strategy:

1. The nature of the home "product" means that good customer service will be an extremely important part of the builder's sales strategy. Considering the cost of the home purchase and the complexity of the product, most home buyers can be expected to be highly sensitive to the risk involved in this purchase, and to have a great deal of emotional involvement in the process. In these situations, building a high level of trust between the customer and the builder is important. The personal involvement that is associated with good customer service is a natural opportunity to build person-to-person relationships that build trust. This confidence in the builder and the builder's various representatives equates to a perception of high quality and greater satisfaction with the product.
2. The homebuilding industry relies heavily on word-of-mouth referrals, and the builder may thrive or fail based on its success in developing refer-

ral business. Customer-service programs should be designed to maximize these highly satisfied customer referrals that help to develop new business as one of the primary contributors that good customer service can make to increase the homebuilder's sales and profits.

3. Studies by Eliant (formerly known as National Survey Systems) have shown that for home sales, high levels of referral business are essential for successful companies, and customers who have enjoyed exceptional service are most likely to become word-of-mouth evangelists for the builder.[15]

4. The high level of emotionalism associated with buying a home suggests there may be a significant level of post-purchase dissonance on the part of the buyer. Given the relatively long home-selection and purchase cycle, this anxiety can start as soon as the purchase decision is made and will extend for some period after the close. The builder will need to provide a high level of service to moderate this negative affect. Without the appropriate level of customer service, small problems can be magnified, resulting in any or all of the potential negative financial outcomes discussed earlier.

5. In the home-purchase process, many different people are involved with whom the customer may interact. Not all will be direct employees of the builder, but they all are likely to be judged by the customer as representative of the quality and concern the builder shows for the customer and the product. It is important for the builder to establish expectations of high standards in customer service with all those employees, subcontractors, salespersons, and other representatives who will come into contact with potential customers.

6. The fact that "people don't complain" means the homebuilder will need to be proactive in asking customers about their satisfaction level throughout the buying cycle, to ensure that any problems are corrected along the way, and that very satisfied customers result from every sale.

7. Providing levels of customer service that consistently exceed customer expectations will allow the builder to command a premium price for the home inventory, and to outdistance competitors by building a reputation for quality that no amount of advertising can overcome.

The Bottom Line on Customer-Service Quality

Quality is often defined as conformance to specification, but this phrase can be misleading. Quality is conformance to *customer* specifications; the customer's definition of quality, not management's, is what counts. To earn a reputation for quality with its customer service, an organization must do more than satisfy needs; it must continually exceed customer expectations.

SERVICE ASSESSMENT

1. Take a serious look at the service strategy in place for your organization by meeting with each department representative. You can accomplish this in either group or one-on-one meetings. Use the following questions to guide your discussions:

   a. What customer service "successes" have you seen in the past year?

   b. What incidents could be considered "wake-up" calls with negative financial impacts?

2. Use the chart below to analyze the impact of poor customer service experiences. How do disappointed customers express their dissatisfaction?

Did the experience cost . . .	Yes	No	Don't Know	Cost
a. Loss of repeat business or loss of ancillary services offered by the builder?				
b. Loss of referral business due to negative word-of-mouth advertising?				
c. Additional advertising, promotional, or public-relations costs to restore corporate image?				
d. Regulatory audits or fines?				
e. Litigation defense or damages settlements?				

3. How will effective customer service programs benefit builders?

The Service Culture

What Is Your Corporate Culture?

I was having dinner one evening with the president of a very successful construction firm in the Midwest. I listened with interest as he explained how his "new" Generation X employees just weren't like the employees of the old days, when the company was first getting started.

"Today's employees don't have the same work ethic. They aren't proactive in solving customer problems, they don't take the initiative to do things on their own, and they don't seem to take responsibility for getting the job done on time and getting it done right. They are constantly letting things fall through the cracks," he said.

In my interaction with many other businesses, most of which are less successful than my friend's, this was a theme I was used to hearing often. Still, I was somewhat surprised to hear this coming from him.

I only had to ask two questions to know that I was on the right track to understanding his problem. The first question was "How do your employees know that you want them to take the initiative?"

He looked straight at me with a puzzled look on his face. "I guess I never really thought about it, but isn't that a natural expectation for anyone who holds a job these days? It's like knowing that you should bathe and shower before coming to work."

My second question was even more puzzling to him. "If I were a potential new employee who was thinking of joining your company, how would you describe the company's values to me?"

After thinking for about 10 seconds, he admitted that these values were difficult to accurately describe in words. He could quickly point to those employees who personify the values—and even those who don't—but *putting the values into words to explain to me or anyone else* was a completely different story. It's a little bit like the Supreme Court arguing over the definition of pornography. The members "can't define it, but they know it when they see it."

When my friend's company was just getting started, the small number of close-knit employees who worked together came from the same background and shared a common set of beliefs about how the company should deal with its customers. Over time, the company had become ever more successful, and the number of employees had continued to grow. What was originally a common set of beliefs shared among close friends had, for lack of a clearly defined corporate philosophy, turned into a range of diverse and individual opinions about how employees should act toward their jobs and their customers.

The point I was making with my friend is this: If you want employees to behave in a certain way, it's probably a good idea not just to assume they know what to do, but instead to communicate to them what the accepted norms and practices are. And if you want to do this in such a way that encourages them to take the initiative in solving problems, you will need to communicate these norms as a guiding company philosophy, not just a set of rules and regulations that may apply only in limited cases.

Most countries have their own distinct cultures that determine how people living there are expected to respond to others and to different situations they might encounter. Within a business context, the same is true of companies. Evolution and environment develop the culture in a country over a number of generations; in a company, the organization's leaders must clearly articulate and show by example what the company's culture is. New employees are in a position somewhat similar to that of visitors to a foreign country. As outsiders setting foot on foreign soil, visitors want to make a positive impression and do the right thing, yet knowing how to act is difficult if everything is totally new and unfamiliar to them.

My first assignment to Indonesia brought this point home very clearly. Although I was excited about the training sessions and meetings that were scheduled with local officials, this was my first trip to a country with business, religious, and social practices quite different from what I was used to, and even the question of what my wardrobe should include created bouts of anxiety for me. Before my trip, I thought I had prepared adequately by studying reference materials from my local bookstore that were supposed to acclimate me to the country's customs and practices. On the flight over, I was confident that the book had covered everything I needed to know, and that I was well prepared. This perspective proved to be completely true, right up until I got off the plane. When I met my host at the airport, he started to greet me with the traditional kiss on both cheeks. Heaving read about the custom, I offered my cheek as well. Unfortunately, when I went to my right, he went to his left. Instead of a warm gesture of good will, the moment became awkward and embarrassing. As we regrouped to start over, he whispered the secret, unfortunately overlooked by my book. "Custom calls for you to always go to the left first," he explained.

I was fortunate that I had a mentor who showed me exactly what was expected, so that I didn't make the same mistake again in my next meetings with some of the country's most influential developers, real-estate brokers, and government officials. For those meetings, I used his critical advice about this and other subtleties of the culture, and everything went smoothly.

New employees don't always have the luxury of a complete corporate indoctrination, or of having a mentor who can coach them through every encounter with customers. They need a formal introduction to the company's belief system, to guide them in performing their jobs and in interacting with customers. Like my friend's company, many businesses haven't taken the time required to develop, or they don't realize the importance of developing, a clearly defined corporate culture, and then communicating this culture with a suitable orientation program to new employees. This lack of a common understanding of the company's goals and values can be a major cause both of inconsistent job performance and of poorly executed customer service, as employees try to find their own framework for how to handle customers.

Had I not had the direction and guidance of my mentor in Indonesia, my only recourse would have been to observe how other people acted and then follow their lead, even if I couldn't completely understand why they were behaving as they did. The situation is similar with new employees. If managers don't provide them with the specific framework of how they want them to perform their jobs and interact with customers, these employees will either look to someone else for guidance or operate from their own perspective. And the self-selected "mentors" are not always the best coaches or role models.

Every company needs to have a clearly defined culture that leaves no doubt about what is expected of each employee. Although most leaders will say that they support a customer-driven culture, what this means in terms of expected employee behavior must be more clearly spelled out. The best way to educate employees about the customer-service role they all must adopt is to establish a clear corporate culture that demonstrates to all employees, without a doubt, what the basic ground rules are when they are representing the company with its customers.

Corporate Culture Defined

What do we really mean when we talk about *corporate culture?* Simply, corporate culture is a system of common beliefs and values everyone who is part of an organization holds. It is a set of core principles that guide and dictate the behaviors of those who play a role in delivering the company's products or services. Most companies have a *mission statement,* but those famous one-sentence explanations of everything the company stands for really only describe what the company wants to be. The *core values* are the "golden rules" of operation that guide employee actions and words. A corporate culture that can be clearly articulated is one that can be passed on to new generations of employees and one that ensures everyone possesses the same set of shared beliefs. In the absence of a clearly defined culture, the opposite happens. Employees and work teams apply their own sets of values and belief systems, based on individual frameworks or experiences.

The builder's world becomes even more complicated because of the number of non-employees, agents, and subcontractors used. Each trade-contracting company, and the individuals who work for that company, may have their own cultures, as well. Sometimes, these views are consistent with the builder's view, but just as often they may be at odds with it. From the customer's view, any of these non-employee groups he or she may interact with also represent the builder, so the builder must find ways for all involved parties to agree with and conform to the standards and culture of the builder.

No one intentionally delivers substandard service, but it often results when there is a lack of standards, or when those standards that the individuals responsible for delivering a service embrace do not match the standards the builder has tried to establish. The result is often a form of service chaos. Without clear-cut guidelines about what is expected, individuals will perform duties based on their own perceptions, which creates a "silo effect" for communication and cooperation, as shown in Figure 2-1. The *silo effect,* sometimes heard in the ranks as the "not my job" syndrome, occurs when organizations, and the employees who represent them, become points at which communication is limited because of a lack of shared values among functional groups. In these environments, individual service approaches are practiced that may or may not be on target to meet the needs of the constituency being served.

The shortfall with this type of thinking is that allowing individual practices to represent company standards for customer service may be as bad as having no standards at all. What is acceptable in one organization may be totally meaningless and irrelevant to the home buyer in the builder's world. With the large number of situations that can arise in day-to-day customer-service delivery, foreseeing every possible occurrence and defining specific rules to cover all these instances is impossible. Instead, companies must establish a "culture of

Figure 2-1 Service Silos

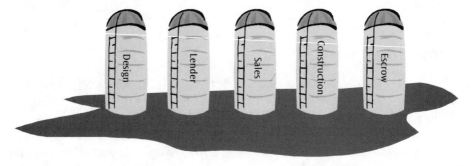

service" that looks at service delivery as part of a system in a synergistic framework that involves all participants. Such a system can capitalize on the good intentions of everyone involved, while it establishes easily understood common values and guidelines for dealing with customers. All service providers can then consistently follow these clear values and guidelines.

So how do builders create a culture of service? The concept is simple, but, as my friend in the construction business found, explaining the culture to others, or putting the concepts down on paper without considerable thought, might not be so easy. Doing so embodies a necessary process of analysis, definition, and strategy development that involves all of the participants that an organization needs to go through to create an effective culture of service throughout the company. This process is defined pictorially in the Service Synergy Model in Figure 2-2.

There is no doubt about the importance of formulating a coherent written description of the organization's service culture. This description not only defines boundaries of conduct, but it also creates an organizational identity, much like a company's product or brand identity, that separates it from other similar services or products. This articulated identity with its accompanying standards of behavior serves a multitude of purposes:

1. It governs hiring decisions, serving as a benchmark for evaluating potential hires to determine which candidates possess the kind of attitudes that fit best with the culture.
2. Similarly, it serves as a useful guideline for evaluating potential partners, allowing for a comparison of cultures to see how well others might fit with the organization.
3. The culture definition provides the social framework for helping new employees assimilate more quickly and integrate smoothly into the organization, using behaviors and actions consistent with those of their longer-tenured colleagues.
4. The shared values ensure that everyone is moving in the same direction, committed to something larger than the independent actions of each individual employee or agent.
5. Finally, a written culture shows trade contractors and other vendors who are part of the building process how dedicated and committed the builder is to customer satisfaction, and it helps them to understand what is expected of them.

Companies that have been effective in establishing strong cultures are easily recognizable, because the behavior of their employees at every level will consistently reflect those corporate values in their interactions with customers.

Creating a Service-Oriented Culture

Most company leaders intuitively believe that delivering good customer service can lead to a competitive advantage for their organizations. Yet, when it comes to making this goal seem achievable to others, the task becomes more difficult. Cultures aren't created by waving a magic wand over a black top hat, or by writing

Figure 2-2 Service Synergy Model

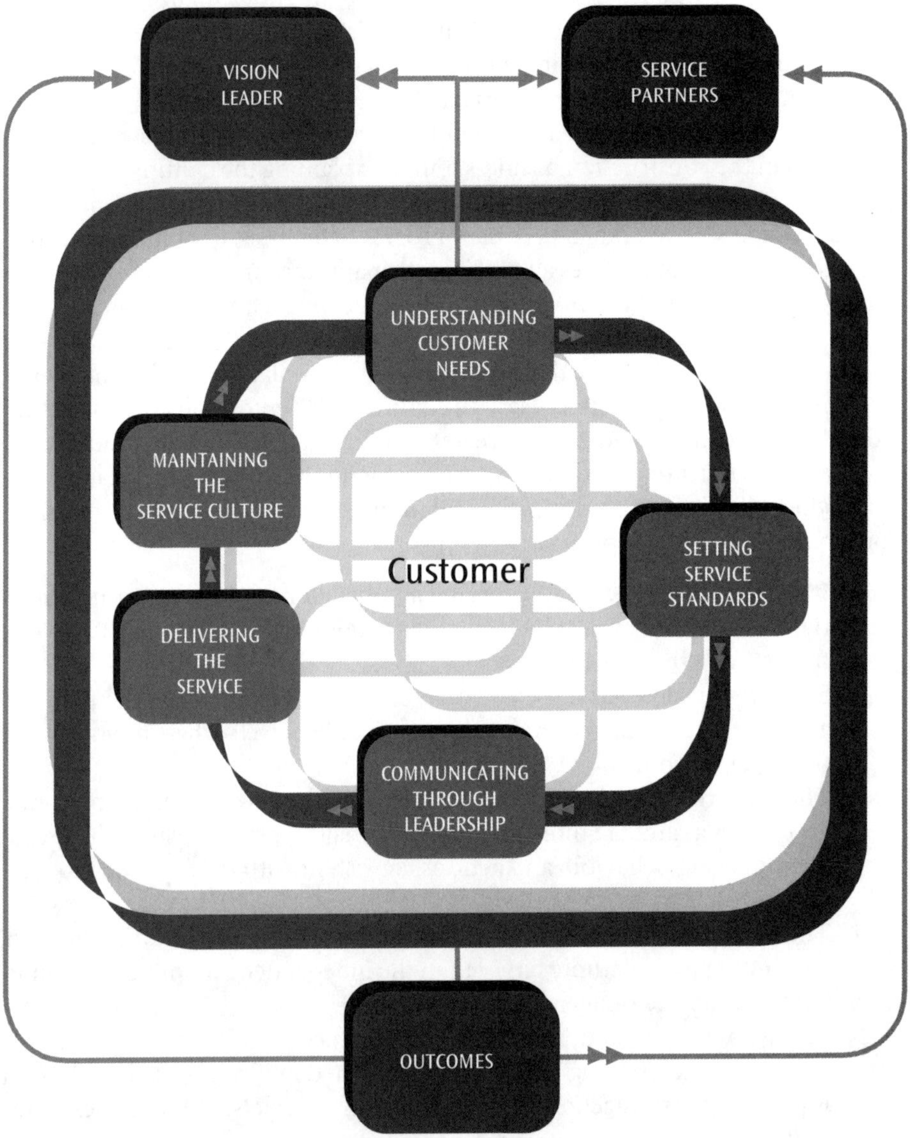

reams of policy manuals. Creating a service-oriented culture when the slate is completely bare can seem daunting. However, if you believe the adage that a picture is worth a thousand words, the Service Synergy Model provides a navigable roadmap. This model shows how to create a service-oriented culture that can help organizations consistently deliver good customer service.

Start with a Vision

The Service Synergy Model defines the actual steps an organization needs to take to implement an effective customer-service culture. Before we start the discussion of these steps, however, several important prerequisites must be in place for successful design and implementation of the service culture. All service initiatives begin with a leader who understands the importance of good customer service to both an organization's customers and its bottom line. Obviously, the ideal situation is one in which everyone in the organization embraces this concept, and that is much more likely to happen when highly visible leaders champion the cause.

The process the Service Synergy Model outlines works just as well for individual workgroups, entire departments, and the overall organization. No matter how large or small the group, someone needs to step forward as the vision leader. This person is the champion of the initiative and firmly believes in the value of embarking on the service voyage. Stephen R. Covey, in his book *The 7 Habits of Highly Effective People,* says it best when he advocates "Begin with the end in mind."[1] Trying to create a service culture without visualizing the end result is like taking a vacation without deciding the final destination. Time will pass, the company won't reach any specific destination, and the route it takes may end up being a tortuous and costly one. The vision is critical because it becomes the foundation on which all other layers are built. The vision is the inspiration behind day-to-day activities, and it ensures that everyone is working toward the same goal.

Guiding principles are the part of the culture that forms a structural framework to dictate how individual service providers will behave. Except in the case of law and ethics, there is no right or wrong set of guiding values. Some companies, such as that of my colleague in the construction industry, are highly entrepreneurial and want their employees empowered to make decisions. Others may require more structure because of the type of products they are dealing with, or they may simply believe in the command-and-control structure wherein everything flows from the top down. The choice of guiding principles is completely at the discretion of the service visionary, consistent with overall corporate values. The challenges inherent in establishing these principles are making sure that existing and future organization members believe in the same set of principles and that they are a match for the organization. Guiding values usually relate to fundamental concepts such as the following:

- Entrepreneurship and innovation
- Risk-taking
- Detail and quality orientation
- Results versus process outcomes
- Concern for people
- Teamwork
- Assertiveness
- Behavior standards and professionalism
- Reward or incentive systems

Service delivery does not happen in a vacuum. In addition to all the internal departments that contribute to service delivery, a multitude of outside people, such as suppliers, vendors, lenders, design firms, attorneys, escrow or settlement officials, and other trade contractors, play an important part in the new-home-purchase cycle. Anyone who performs a task related to the delivery of service to the ultimate customer becomes a representative of the builder and, in effect, a service partner. If a service partner fails in any way, whether with defective parts, appliances, incomplete inventories, or missed deadlines, the customer's service experience can be adversely affected, with the builder ultimately bearing the responsibility for the customer's dissatisfaction.

The fact that the "buck" always stops at the builder's door does not mean, however, that the builder should design the guiding principles in complete isolation. Strategies driven from the top down without input from those who play a significant role in service delivery are at the greatest risk of failure. Fortunately, builders have a number of service partners to draw from, and they should take full advantage of these partners as they develop guiding principles and standards for service delivery.

Including representatives from these groups in the early stages of culture development lays the foundation for open and honest communication, creates buy-in from service providers, and helps to diminish future misunderstandings about builders' service expectations. Chris Saunders, as Director of Facilities with the Bank of Hawaii, did just that when he took over direction of the facilities group. To strengthen the relationship with service partners, Saunders invited key vendors to the same customer-service training as that provided for direct employees. This approach became the first step in breaking down communication barriers and demonstrating the willingness to create a more partner-oriented relationship. He then went on to establish weekly team meetings between staff and contractors, often looking to them for help with creative solutions to problems that surfaced along the way. This open communication line invited suggestions from those directly involved in the delivery, allowing service levels to be improved and costs reduced by drawing on the expertise and commitment of experienced partners.

The time spent in establishing strong working relationships at the start ultimately paves the way for a smoother path to vision implementation. Bringing the participants who are actually responsible for delivering service into the discussion, for consensus decisions, makes sure that participants provide their own input into the process, and also increases the likelihood that they will have a strong buy-in to the policies they were at least partly responsible for defining. Everyone can better work together to focus on the customer-service vision that will meet the overall needs of the builder and the home buyers when partners are recognized and involved as part of the builder's team.

How important it is to choose service partners carefully because of their role in representing you with customers, like your own employees do, is worth restating. Outside service partners should share the same values and subscribe to the same standards as your company embraces; otherwise, the different groups can be continuously working at cross-purposes, with the customer caught in the middle. Like a well-fitting suit, everything should match and fit together properly to make the best impression on the customer.

The day a telephone company telemarketer called me, I was reminded of how important the choice of service partners can be. My name obviously was on his calling list from a new airline frequent-flyer program that I had enrolled in two months before the call. From the tone of the telemarketer's voice, I could sense his enthusiasm to promote his product and make the sale. He no doubt sat in front of his computer monitor reading from the script that would ensure he said all the right things to entice me to change telephone companies. I patiently listened to his pitch as he explained how switching to his telephone company would give me an opportunity to accumulate more frequent-flier miles and take even more trips to places I wanted to go. At the end, he asked his closing question, designed to get me to immediately make the move: "Can we sign you up today?"

Now was my chance to talk. "You know, I don't usually fly that airline, but on that trip I was going to a destination more easily accessible by that airline's routing, so I signed up for its frequent-flier program. For the first time in 15 years of regular flying, my luggage was lost; leaving me without a business suit for the seminar I was attending the next morning. Not only did the airline lose my luggage, but it took four days to find it, and in the process I received the worst customer service I have ever experienced in my entire life. I will never fly that airline again."

Apparently, there was nothing in the script to cover this response. The telemarketer tried for a quick recovery by pointing out the other airlines the company was affiliated with, which were just as good as the first one he'd mentioned, but by that time it was too late. After singing the praises of the first airline as his company's important new partner, the company was now losing credibility by offering frequent-flier mileage on other airlines that weren't even a part of the original call. I already had a bad impression of the initial airline, and now I was inclined to put his telephone company in the same category as its favored partner. The moral of the story is this: Select partners carefully, because they become a representative of your organization in front of the customer, and you will ultimately be judged by the company you keep.

Key Steps in Creating a Service Culture

With the vision and service partners in place, the builder is ready to begin implementing the five key steps of the Service Synergy Model. Directing the successful completion of these steps with the service partners is the builder's most important task. The five steps are the following:

1. **Understanding customer needs through research.** This step ensures that the builder is clearly identifying the true customers and their needs, using multiple analysis methods. Who are your "real" customers? That question should be relatively simple to answer. Yet, sometimes it is more difficult than you might think. Builders must respond to many different constituencies with uniquely different needs. So understanding what their real customers actually need from them can be a challenge. Different strokes for different folks was never truer than it is today.

Superior customer service is a matter of meeting customers' needs and exceeding their expectations. To do this, you must know what these requirements are—not what you *think* they are. How do you determine your customers' needs and expectations? The simple answer is to ask them, and then listen closely to what they are saying, so that you can take appropriate action. In practice, a more rigorous approach, using targeted research methods, is needed to fully understand and prioritize the needs of a large and diverse customer base.

Attempting to create a customer-service culture without using targeted research is highly risky and usually an invitation to failure. We all like to think we know our customers, but there are usually serious limits to this knowledge, especially when it comes to problems areas that customers are less inclined to discuss directly with us as their service provider. There are a number of ways, both formal and informal, to gather valid information about customer needs.

Too often, companies will conduct research, but they use a relatively small and limited sample size, or even a single focus group, and they base their future strategies on those responses. This limited feedback may be biased and not representative of what the builder's more complete customer base actually needs. Because customer expectations and performance standards are constantly changing, the key is to continually monitor the needs and satisfaction levels of constituents.

2. **Setting service standards.** The next step is to create the actual performance standards, based on the important customer requirements identified in step 1. Effective research efforts will provide guidance in this area. When clearly written, service standards serve as measurable guidelines for delivering service with consistency and at a level that pleases all customers who come in contact with the builder's personnel and representatives.

Because of the complexity of the building process and the number of service partners involved, territorial barriers, or functional "silos" (as in Figure 2-2) can easily surface. Combine external silos with those that might exist internally—departments that act autonomously rather than as a synergistic part of the total organization—and the formula is in place for miscommunication and service failures on many levels. Bringing service partners in early to collaborate on the establishment of service standards lays the groundwork for open communication and problem solving rather than finger pointing and blame when those inevitable service failures do occur.

3. **Communicating through leadership.** Ask front-line service providers what the number-one problem is in their organizations, and the answer will overwhelmingly be lack of communication. The importance of good communication between companies, their customers, trade contractors, and employees seems so obvious that it should not be necessary to mention it. Even though communication is the most important element in the process of building and maintaining relationships, it is also the one ele-

ment most frequently absent from customer-service initiatives. This recurring theme echoes repeatedly throughout corporate America. With all of the technology and telecommunication devices available today, it's hard to believe that communication would be a major problem.

Initially, the service standards themselves are what get communicated. However, those written standards must be backed by actions that demonstrate the continued commitment to quality service that the service culture defines.

Good communication starts internally, with the organization's leadership. Because communication is a complex process, barriers and breakdowns can easily occur, which can lead to service failures when two-way communication is hampered in some way. To counter this, formal procedures for ensuring regular communication at various milestones in the service-delivery process should be defined as part of this step.

4. **Delivering the service.** Once the service standards are established and communicated both internally and externally, it's up to the service providers to do what they do best—deliver the service. Putting the first three steps in place will prepare providers for delivering the quality service first visualized. However, continual monitoring is still needed to ensure that no unforeseen obstacles get in the way of service delivery. The best service strategy can falter without employees who are dedicated to delivering the best service possible.

5. **Maintaining the service culture.** The final step is the one that probably most requires builders to demonstrate their leadership abilities. In comparison to creating a service culture, keeping it alive with empowered and motivated employees is probably the most difficult task. Employees will perform beyond expectations in this role if the environment is created in which they are appropriately rewarded for their efforts and can grow as important contributors to the company's success.

Summary

An organization's culture develops over time, usually starting with the founders because they had an original vision of what their company should be and how it should deal with its customers. At the start, the slate is clean, and the founders are unconstrained by history or carry-over "baggage" from a previous management team. The company's small size in the beginning allows the founders to easily communicate their vision to everyone who is part of the organization. As the company grows, communication becomes more difficult, and establishing a more defined culture of service is essential to make sure the diverse employee base understands and adopts the cultural ground rules the founders have set. Founders must depend on others to reinforce the culture and to carry on the traditions they established early on. Like the game of "Telephone" children play, the message becomes diluted as it is repeated by one person after another, unless the culture is well documented and established within the organization. Keeping the culture alive is possible by hiring the right people, thoroughly acclimating them to the culture through training, and rewarding and reinforcing those who demonstrate exemplary service practices in support of the corporate service. Through the builder's diligence and proactive leadership, internal employees, trade contractors, and other service partners can consistently maintain the service culture and deliver excellent service. With leadership and vision in establishing a culture of service, the builder will have created a seamless standard for excellence whereby employees and partners alike can consistently provide good customer service.

SERVICE ASSESSMENT

1. What is the importance of a customer-driven culture?
2. Briefly describe the Service Synergy Model for culture development.
3. What are the five steps to creating a culture of service?

What Customers Expect from Us

What Do You Expect from Your Airline?

One Sunday, I was flying from the West Coast to Harrisburg, Pennsylvania. Although I have a tendency to use one airline more than another, this time I decided to try a different one with more direct routing. As a frequent flier, I was curious to see how this airline would compare to my favorite. Checking in at the counter, I was greeted by an agent who had the uncanny ability to verify my identification, pull up my reservation, give me a seat assignment, and check my baggage, all in less than 20 seconds. Before the words were out of my mouth to ask, she informed me, without even checking her terminal, that there were no aisle seats available, only center. Her apparent efficiency was amazing.

Making my way to the gate and waiting for my row to be called, I observed the passing stream of roll-on bags my fellow passengers were carrying aboard ahead of me. Of course, by the time I boarded, there was no overhead space for my laptop computer, purse, and winter coat, and no offer of help from the flight attendants. My body squeezed into the center seat that would be my home for the next few hours and, fortunately, I was able to navigate myself into a semi-comfortable position, at least until the passenger in front of me put his seat back in my lap, locking me into position. Scalp massage anyone? As the doors were closing,

I noted a number of passengers moving to still-available aisle seats to make themselves more comfortable for the flight.

The snack bag that had been tossed my way helped to take my mind off the cramped seating, at least until the unannounced turbulence bounced most of the items off my tray and sent me scrambling to avoid spilling my drink in my lap. Never had I been so glad to get back on the ground. By the time I got to the baggage claim area, the circulation had nearly resumed in my legs. Stretching felt so good that I didn't notice until the baggage area was nearly deserted that I was the only one still waiting for luggage.

The gentleman standing at the airline's baggage desk looked the other way as I approached and started explaining that my luggage was not with the flight. He gave me a knowing look and advised that it is not unusual for luggage to be delayed until the next flight. If my luggage was on the plane, it would be delivered to my hotel by ten o'clock that evening. I was relieved, knowing that I had to stand in front of 30 seminar attendees at eight o'clock the next morning, and I needed to be dressed in fresh business attire.

After I followed the usual routine of checking into the hotel and having dinner, I placed a call to the baggage-claim representative to see whether, in fact, my luggage was on the last plane. As I had feared, it was not. The operator, who I questioned about what to do to weather this major inconvenience, offered no helpful suggestions, but she did provide an extensive laundry list of don'ts. "Don't do anything for 24 hours. Don't buy any merchandise because you will not be reimbursed for it. Don't call us again until five o'clock in the morning, and then we will let you know what to do." That response set the pattern often repeated over the next four days. While I tried to get some kind of answer about what happened, more than a dozen different people uttered some of the most idiotic responses, and each person seemed to give me progressively worse service. Combined with all the other events that occurred during my trip at the hands of this company, my fury increased along with the vow that the president of the airline, in probably one of the last contacts I would ever have with this company, would hear about his customer "disservice" department.

I understand that seats fill up, computers go down, agents get busy, and luggage gets lost on occasion, even though, in more than 15 years of flying, this was the first time it had happened to me. Most perplexing was the extremely poor treatment I received from virtually everyone associated with this company— employees who, from my experience, did not seem to care a bit how they treated their customers.

After I had spent several hundred dollars for replacement clothes and offered apologies to my clients for the disruption, I successfully finished the seminars. When I inquired at check-in for my return trip home, the agent confirmed there was still no news about the lost luggage. I was halfway to the security checkpoint when my name was paged over the loudspeaker. I made my way back to the passenger desk and was surprised to hear the same ticket agent tell me they had now found my luggage. Yes, after all this time, they found my baggage in Hartford, Connecticut. Evidently, the original ticket agent, who turned out to not be so efficient after all, put the wrong tags on my baggage, sending it on a special journey to a destination alphabetically near, but geographically far, from my destination. The agent gave her assurance that my baggage would be returned by five o'clock the next day.

Sure enough, the next day around midnight my doorbell rang, rousing me from a deep sleep. There, sitting on my front step, was my luggage, in much better condition than its owner. It had finally come home, after a much more interesting and relaxed trip than my own.

What Customers Expect from Us

How would you say the airline performed in terms of meeting my needs? Well, it did get me from one coast to the other and back again, which was the actual service I originally paid for. If no luggage had been involved, this service may have passed as average or at least marginally acceptable. But all of my inter- actions with people or things that represented the airline had left me unhappy with the product and determined not to use that company again. That good customer service encompasses more than the basic product purchase is well established. To deliver good customer service and to do so efficiently, we must understand what customers really need from us:

- What do customers expect from the product and the people selling, serv- icing, and otherwise supporting that product?
- Who, inside or outside the organization, is best equipped to satisfy those needs?
- Under what circumstances or in what situations can we expect to come face-to-face with customers' requirements?

Defining the Service Experience

In the example above, a number of well-defined needs obviously came about through my purchase and use of the product (i.e., airline travel). That purchase resulted in ample opportunities for the airline to succeed or fail in satisfying this range of needs, which I expected it to provide based on our contract. Ulti- mately, my decision to continue to use and recommend this company to others in the future depended on how well my needs and expectations were satisfied throughout the entire delivery process.

Service usually falters, and hence dis- satisfaction occurs, when the service provider must play a role that goes beyond the customer's basic needs.

My basic needs were met when the reservation was made, the financial transaction occurred, and the transportation service was provided to get me to my destination. However, my expectations were also that the airline would take steps to make me reasonably comfortable during my travel, would transport my luggage to the same destination, would accommodate reasonable requests, and would treat me with courtesy and consideration. Unfortunately, very few of those expectations were met. Service usually falters, and hence dissatisfaction occurs, when the service provider must play a role that goes beyond the customer's basic needs.

In this experience, the agent, the flight attendants, and the baggage and customer service representatives, among others, seemed ill equipped or else unmotivated to use their communication and problem-resolution skills to satisfy my expectations. Even the pilot's failure to announce the approaching turbulence, which nearly spilled my drink, contributed to my impression. At the very least, an acknowledgement of the uncomfortable ride would have soothed my already jangled nerves. Most people do not realize how significant the interaction with a customer can be at each of these critical events. Performance at these turning points can mean either ultimate success or failure for any service-oriented business.

In the example above, the service that company representatives provided at each contact with them helped me form an opinion of the company, its product, how it values customers, and how important customer service is to its business. My impression alone will potentially mean the difference of hundreds of thousands of travel dollars not spent with this company and instead directed to its competitors in the future. Ironically, given my profession, I end up repeating this story often; in front of audiences I am coaching on the importance of good customer service, as a perfect example of how not to treat customers.

Drivers of Customer Satisfaction

When we as customers purchase a product or service, we do so with the belief that the features, specifications, and characteristics of the product, as presented, will satisfy the requirements we have for the product. Ideally, when common specifications (as both the service provider and the customer understand them) are met, the customer's original set of motivations or needs for acquiring the product will have been satisfied. In practice, however, there may be considerable interpretation of specifications on both sides, and these interpretations can lead to different customer expectations about what will actually be received. When there is a shortfall between what customers think they are getting and what they receive, this expectations differential can create a new "need" that must be addressed, to correct for the perceived product deficiency or service failure.

For example, the airline promised to get me to the East Coast, which is what I needed. However, in the process of receiving this service, I experienced a trip laced with incidents that inconvenienced me, cost me time and money, and made the journey more difficult than I had anticipated. My expectation was to be comfortable, to retain my luggage, to have reasonable requests treated with courtesy and efficiency, and to not be unduly inconvenienced. Few of these expectations were met. I now had to obtain and be compensated for replacement clothes and delivery service to bring my luggage to a destination other than the airport, both new needs I originally did not have.

When a customer purchases a product or service, basic needs and expectations are implicit in the purchase agreement between that customer and the service provider. This includes expectations about how any service should be accomplished. When well defined and clearly explained to the customer, the product itself will, in most cases, fulfill the basic needs that motivated the customer to purchase in the first place. The customer-service function will more likely be one of dealing with less-well-defined or implicit customer expectations, which by nature may have as much to do with how the product or service is provided than with the product itself. In fact, many of these expectations may not become apparent from discussions with the customer until they are later not realized and so result in customer complaints. To achieve desirable high-satisfaction levels, what customers need from us is, of course, to have these basic needs met. However, we must also satisfy customers' less-well-defined expectations every time an interaction occurs between them and our company or its representatives.

The customer experience is affected in two other areas beyond the product and its performance. The company's internal support processes and its practices for handling customer relationships can affect the outcome of the customer's experience. When I tried to obtain some kind of assistance with emergency-replacement articles for my lost luggage, the airline's customer-service representative could only parrot to me things that could not be done. These internal policies and procedures were designed to keep unhappy customers from taking undue advantage of the airline. However, the manner in which she delivered this news made the situation even worse. Her ability to take me from disappointment to full-blown anger in a matter of seconds created in me even more dissatisfaction with the airline. When expectations have not been met, customers naturally feel a sense of disappointment. And how customer-service representatives handle customer disappointment will either enhance loyalty or escalate the disappointment into anger, as shown in Figure 3-1.

So when an organization is looking at ways to meet customer expectations, it must examine the total infrastructure for any weaknesses. Figure 3-2 shows how controlling quality of service in all four areas—product, service performance, internal support processes, and customer relations—will add value to the customer's experience and differentiate one provider from another. Without that differentiation, the only other way for the customer to make a distinction is with price.

Figure 3-1 Stages of Customer Feelings

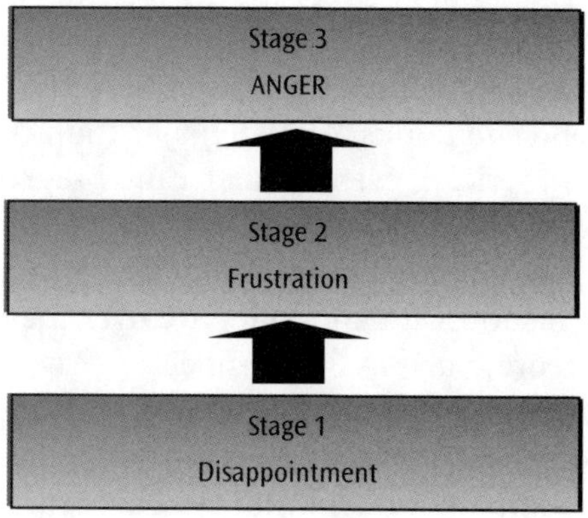

AVOID CREATING UNREASONABLE EXPECTATIONS:
TIPS FOR EFFECTIVELY SAYING NO

Service providers may inadvertently upset their customers or even escalate an already difficult situation if the providers cannot give customers something they want or have been led to believe they can receive. This situation is especially difficult if the expectations were not due to misunderstanding, but instead resulted from unrealistic promises that had been made previously, and which must be contradicted later. Setting unreasonable or misleading expectations initially and later breaking that commitment is one of the greatest contributors to the service-performance gap that home buyers experience today.

Providing accurate information about what is possible up front is better than creating unrealistic expectations. When you are faced with unreachable customer goals, there are, however, better ways to say No than rejecting customer requests outright. The next time you are faced with this challenge, try these alternatives:

- Give customers other options by offering what can be done before saying what cannot be done.

- Explain why the request is not possible because of policies, product limitations, building code restrictions, or other circumstances.

- Refer customers to a higher-level authority if the request is beyond your area of responsibility.

Service on the Decision Track

To better understand the connections between customers and the different people who play a part in the delivery of the product or service, it is important to be aware of all the steps that may occur along the way. From the time potential customers identify a desire for a product or service and start down the path toward making a decision about that product, certain opportunities for customer interaction arise. These interaction opportunities become *critical contact points (CCPs)* on the track customers follow to their decision about a product or vendor. Customers form opinions about the organization and the people representing it based on the impressions they receive at each point in the process. Graphically, we can diagram the major opportunities for interaction along a circular path with start and end points. At each major contact point, certain activities may have their own series of events, which can be represented by additional circles as subsets of the main decision track. Every service an employee or company representative delivers, no matter how large or small, has a number of opportunities for interaction with and influence over the customer, and these opportunities can be represented in this manner.

The starting point on the decision track, as seen in Figure 3-3, and the first opportunity for customer interaction begins as soon as customers are exposed to the name of your company or community. This exposure can be through

Figure 3-2 Service Drivers

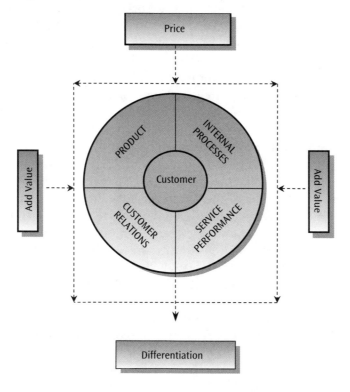

Figure 3-3 Decision-Track Diagram and Critical Contact Points

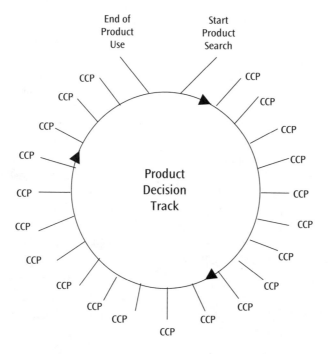

word-of-mouth referral, advertising or marketing media, or any other means. The concluding point on the circle may not occur until long after the purchase is complete, and the product is at end of life. Every time a critical contact occurs, customers form an opinion about the company from that event. Although a number of reinforcing positive events usually are required to achieve a high level of satisfaction with customers, unfortunately, only one negative contact might negate the other points on the circle. Left unresolved, a negative interaction can paint an inaccurate picture of the entire organization and ultimately drive customers to a competitor.

A single sufficiently positive or negative critical contact during the pre-purchase, product-selection period can truly be a critical or fatal event. An impressionable negative event might mean that all the promotion and positive image development that led the customers to consider the product up to this point has been wasted, as the negative event dispels the positive perception of the product and convinces customers to look elsewhere. Conversely, a highly positive event during this time may reinforce customers' already-positive image of the product and convince them to move forward with a purchase decision without looking further. The pre-purchase period is an especially important time to be aware of critical contact points. Interactions that occur after customers have purchased the product can be equally important in retaining satisfied customers who will be repeat users and reliable referral sources to recommend new business. Understanding when these critical contacts might occur and ensuring that the customer-service organization is prepared to support customers at these critical times are the final keys to understanding what they want from us.

Service Delivery Zones

It is obvious that the provider must address both customer needs and customer expectations to achieve success with the service experience. How effectively the provider accomplishes this determines the level of satisfaction customers will derive from the efforts. Figure 3-4 shows four significant result categories, or zones, that providers can expect from the service experience. The service provider's objective is to achieve results that consistently fall into the fourth category, in which needs are met and expectations are exceeded.

The main objective, or need, is obviously to deliver a product or complete an agreed-upon task. In the service execution, there are expectations about how this should be achieved. Within this set of expectations, a subset of needs or expectations exists that drives the satisfaction level. This set of expectations relating to handling customers is so fundamental in virtually all service situations that it could be referred to as customers' "Bill of Rights." This list represents needs and minimum expectations that customers will most likely have for any customer-service experience. These needs and expectations will be true consistently, even though the relative importance of the values changes from one situation to the next. Figure 3-5 lists these core expectations that are the foundation of the customer-vendor relationship and that should be the basis for any effective customer-service program.

Figure 3-4 Service Delivery Zones

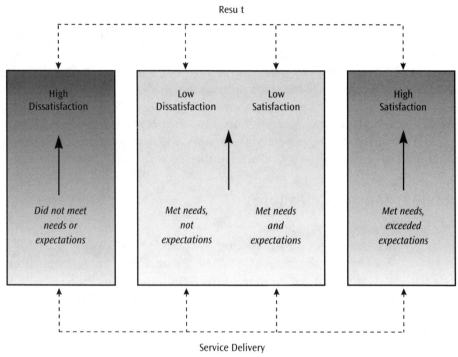

Who Is the "Us" When It Comes to Providing Customer Service?

Before we can talk about what customers expect from "us," we need to clarify whom we are talking about when we refer to "us." One problem in providing customer service is determining which people will be in the best position to engage in and provide the type of service the customer wants. For most companies, the "us" part of the equation involves almost anyone who may meet with

Figure 3-5 Customer Service "Bill of Rights"

Customer Need	Description
Prompt communication	Customers expect to be able to make initial contact with a knowledgeable product representative and receive a satisfactory reply with a minimum delay.
Access to empowered staff	Customers expect any problems to be referred to a level with appropriate authority to resolve them promptly.
Accurate status and information	Customers should have free access to product information, problem status, or other detail needed to resolve issues.
Courtesy and consideration	The representative should show due respect for customers.
Corrective-action options	Available choices to resolve problems should be presented to customers.
Reliable execution	Promises or commitments made should be honored.

customers to represent the product during the entire selection, purchase, delivery, and support process. In many cases, this person may include direct employees as well as authorized or "proxy" representatives for the product who are outside the immediate control of the organization. The homebuilding industry is an extreme case of this complexity, whereby a number of different organizations, trade contractors, and independent salespeople may be the contacts who establish the image of the builder's product at these critical opportunities for service. To expect a certain level of performance from direct employees, over whom one has good control, is one thing; but to expect such performance from outside employees or independent contractors, who have only a partially vested interest in the organization's product, is entirely another situation.

Reasons for Service Failures

It is not difficult to envision how service failures can occur, given the many variables customers and providers encounter in sales of more costly and complex products. Even within the best-intentioned organization, ample opportunities exist for poor communication, misunderstandings, and incorrect specifications, any of which can create unrealistic expectations and dissatisfaction for customers.

Clearly, independent contractors or other outside representatives might represent special problems for the builder in maintaining a high quality of customer service. The often-limited control over non-employee representatives who are involved with the customer makes it difficult to provide adequate training and motivation that will ensure that quality standards the builder has set can be maintained in every customer-service situation. But even the best employees, who may be highly skilled and well-trained, still cannot mitigate the negative effects of a poorly designed customer-service system in which management has shown a lack of understanding of customer requirements or devoted only limited focus to the service function.

One of the more difficult and stressful jobs in a company can be that of the customer-service or -support representatives, who hear complaints all day from unhappy customers, and who must do their best to satisfy these customers with the resources available to them. When these employees are limited by policies that do not allow them the latitude to address the customer's problems, and when they lack the necessary authority to provide what the customer needs, they may fail in their primary task. This failure can lead to frustration and the expression of open complaints about the system to customers and other business associates, which compounds the problem and does even more harm to the product image in customers' minds. Figure 3-6 shows some of the more common reasons for service failures.

The Service-Performance Gap

Typically, management of successful companies has figured out what customers want, tried to prepare staff, and set the policies needed—either formally or

Figure 3-6 Common Reasons for Service Failures

- Poorly defined product specifications.
- Customers are unknowledgeable and ill-informed about certain requirements.
- Manufacturer's marketing efforts and materials described the product inaccurately.
- Sales staff create unrealistic expectations.
- Either customer or vendor make actual mistakes in specification, or there is significant miscommunication and misunderstanding between the vendor and the customer.

informally—to provide what's wanted and needed. Even so, customer satisfaction levels may still fall short of the objectives. The difference between service specifications and the actual service-satisfaction level can be called the *service-performance gap.*

Although the bar may be set low enough that providing acceptable levels of customer service in cases of basic, commodity-like products is easy, the same cannot be said for the majority of products and services. Unfortunately, service-performance gaps involving more sophisticated products, and when the product itself is a service, are common in organizations. Businesses offering services that are highly interactive, labor-intensive, and performed in multiple locations are especially vulnerable to this problem.

Similarly, there tends to be higher variation among service outcomes in labor-intensive services than when service delivery is fully automated. For example, bank customers who use human tellers will experience far more service variation than those using automatic teller machines. With the latter, after customer usage methods, needs, and expectations are determined from the feedback of initial users, the bank can correct any identified problems for subsequent users with design changes to the hardware and software, so the problems do not recur.

There are many opportunities for things to go wrong when service providers and customers interact as freely as is expected in person-to-person service situations. Both parties have ample opportunity to experience and respond to each other's mannerisms, attitude, competence, mood, dress, language, and so forth, responses that ultimately are reflected in the customers' overall satisfaction with the service performed.

In situations in which "service" is the product being delivered, specifications typically may be less well defined and more likely conveyed verbally through some consultative and interactive process. The personal dialogue sets expectations, which are further influenced by the interaction between provider and customer, and by their personalities. Finally, decentralized service production through a chain of outlets complicates quality control because the service provider is more independent and removed from the management and monitoring point.

When a service failure occurs, a flurry of attention after a foul-up may ultimately satisfy that particular customer, but the goal for most organizations should be to establish an underlying infrastructure and culture that consistently makes memorable service possible with every customer, and thus avoids the high cost and risk of constant recovery efforts. Customers certainly appreciate a smiling service representative, but the unseen support systems are usually what get the job done on a regular basis. The right combination of policies, well-trained staff, and technology applied to satisfying the customer can give an organization a powerful strategic advantage over its competitors.

Critical Contacts for Service on the Decision Track

Good customer service should satisfy both the well-defined needs and more subjective expectations that customers have. When management has done its job right, the systems and people will be in place to provide the service that customers expect. The training and policies the company has established for dealing with customers will address the main reasons for service failures. But with these resources and procedures operating effectively, one other very important aspect to any organization's customer-service program is most often overlooked. That aspect is the "when" of customer service.

Most organizations anticipate the obvious situations in which customers will expect service, but for any service program to be successful, they must also establish a culture that can address customer requirements for service at virtually every customer encounter, even those that may not have been anticipated. Many more chances for interaction with customers occur at critical contact points, at which service is important to shaping customers' impressions of a product or service, than most people realize. Preparing for these unanticipated service events as part of a total service-delivery system is an important factor in avoiding serious service-performance gaps in an otherwise sound customer-service program.

What Customers Want from the Builder

The home buyer is certainly expected to demand a high level of customer service. The problems the builder faces in providing this level of service encompass virtually all of the issues described above. However, two concepts are especially important for the builder's markets. The critical-contact-point concept highlights the fact that the builder's job of customer service starts long before customers may come face-to-face with the builder's product or representatives. Figure 3-7 shows some of the more common contact points that customers will encounter in the typical home-buying cycle.

Critical contact points for the builder will probably start with potential homebuyers' first attempts to look at prospective neighborhoods. They may do this alone, or, more likely, with a real estate agent. The buyers continue from there with a series of indeterminate events during the shopping phase, from which they form an impression about the builder's product. The fact that most of these contacts are not with direct employees of the builder means that the builder will have to rely on influence and persuasion to ensure that the contacts

**Figure 3-7 Home-Buying
Decision Track**

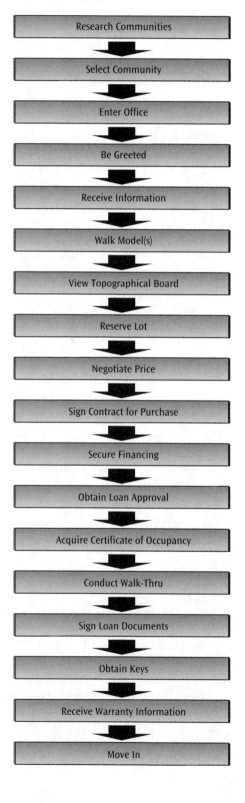

represent the product well in the service they provide to the customers. Especially when a number of new home builders are represented in the same area, it is important for builders to distinguish their products from the competition through these independent service providers.

What does this situation imply about any overall program the builder might put in place to provide highest quality service to customers? Regardless of the allegiance or responsibility to the original product provider of these potential participants in the customer-service interaction, the provider must find appropriate ways to ensure that each is adequately prepared and motivated to represent the product with the customer. Regular use of seminars, open houses, and incentives for agents involved in the process are all ways to accomplish this. Preparing appropriate sales tools and collateral, and making these readily available to these same people, are also useful. Given the technology orientation of today's buyers, a well-designed website with useful information about the products and communities in which they are located is another service that most buyers have come to expect and appreciate. By adding a restricted section to this website that contains useful information for the various service providers, the builder can use this same tool to help get up-to-date information and sales tools to these providers. Such a section will give the providers something unique that also helps to build their loyalty to the builder.

Regardless of the relationship the various agents have with the builder, the builder must constantly audit their performance and the process they are involved in for consistency with the service standards the builder has set, to ensure that customer expectations are being met. The various research methods discussed in the following chapter are useful for regularly monitoring this performance, and they are especially important when the builder's control over these agents is limited.

Lying beneath these critical contact points is the builder's infrastructure that binds everything together, all in an effort to meet, and hopefully exceed, customers' expectations. Obviously, the product itself must meet the standards the customers already have in mind. This means that all systems related to the product, including electrical, heating and air conditioning, plumbing, and lighting, must work perfectly. Any defect the customers find raises the suspicion that quality has been compromised in other areas, too.

With so many individuals involved in the decision track, coordination among critical contact points requires the highest level of communication and synergy. All support and ancillary services, including the design center, lenders, escrow and title officers, attorneys, and after-move-in customer service, must coordinate their efforts to create a seamless service experience for customers.

Customers' first impressions at these critical contact points are always lasting impressions. There may not be a second chance to create a positive image. That is why all customer-contact people need to possess the service-performance skills necessary for keeping customers interested in continuing the relationship with the service provider. Each contact either reinforces customers' decisions as being the right ones or creates doubt about whether they should move forward. Finally, the last brick in the service infrastructure foundation requires that all service providers know how to go above and beyond to meet or exceed customer expectations. Meeting commitments, honoring promises, and being honest and straightforward will help cement the relationship between builder and customer.

Summary

Satisfying customers requires that we meet their basic needs and exceed their expectations for the product or service we are providing. Needs are usually associated with clearly defined specifications that state what the product or service is or does. Expectations are likely to consist of more subjective concepts customers have relating to both the process of providing a product or service, and to less-well-defined aspects of the product specifications. There are many more opportunities for satisfying customer needs and expectations, any or all of which can be critical contact points at which we can either close sales and build long-term customer loyalty, or alienate customers and drive them to competitors. An effective customer-service program needs to do its best to prepare all of the people who might represent the product to do the best possible job of meeting needs and exceeding customer expectations at any of these critical events. The organization can achieve its greatest success by preparing for critical contacts with effective goals, training, motivation, and communication with employees or representatives who are responsible for providing good customer service at each of these opportunities for positively influencing the customer.

SERVICE ASSESSMENT

1. What do customers expect from us?
2. What are some reasons for service failures?
3. What are critical contact points on the decision track?

Better Understanding with Customer Research

How Can We Best Meet Your Needs?

I arrived at my hotel just slightly before the designated check-in time. Trying to be helpful, the front-desk representative graciously looked to see whether there might be a room available. As he tapped his keyboard and stared at the monitor, the furrow in his brow told me he was having difficulty. "I'm sorry, but the only thing we have available right now is a room next to the elevator. Would you like that?"

Being extremely security conscious, I suggested that, because I was traveling alone, I would prefer something in the middle of the hall. He nodded his head in understanding and stated, "I'm sure by the time you come back we will have something a little quieter." It was now my turn to be amazed. Didn't he hear me? Wasn't he listening? Didn't he know that corner rooms by elevators represented the highest security hazards because of their easy access for intruders? Surely the hotel training covers these kinds of things.

Imagine my surprise when I finally reached my destination that would be home for the next two nights. Not only was my room located in a corner by the elevator, but it also was tucked away in its own tiny alcove at the end of a long, dark hallway. So much for my expecting the front-desk person to understand what is important to the customer!

Satisfied customers are an essential prerequisite for any successful business. This statement might sound elementary, but even if we are among the most highly effective organizations, we need to remind our staffs of this fact periodically, especially when they must encounter those "special" customers whose primary mission seems to be to make our jobs harder and our work days more trying. These "special" customers just don't act the way we want them to! They burden us with their complaints and keep us from getting important work done!

Satisfied customers are an essential prerequisite for any successful business.

As incredible as it may seem, some employees in every company still believe customers really are an imposition that gets in the way of accomplishing their "normal" job activities. This perspective can be especially true of operations or line departments that don't typically interact with customers daily, and where customer requests tend to fall outside the routine responsibilities defined for these groups.

Very few companies would suggest we keep only the easy-going customers and discard the rest. Because every viable business plan dedicates many pages to strategies that will be used to attract this precious commodity, we must make sure that we minimize the number of customers falling into that "special" category described above. We can do this by understanding our customers and knowing what they might expect from various groups within our organization, so that everyone can be better prepared to satisfy customers' expectations about the product or service. The hotel agent in the opening monologue should have been aware that security is very important to single women customers; that knowledge would have allowed him to be more responsive to my "specific" needs. If we know what customers' expectations will be and are prepared to satisfy those expectations, "special" customer stories will rarely be heard in our organization.

Any attempt to attract customers, keep them satisfied, and build long-term loyalty is guaranteed to fail if we don't have a good understanding of those customers' characteristics, and what they are looking for from the product and service we are expected to provide. For this reason, the first few questions an organization should try to answer are "Who are your customers, and what do they really want from you, your product, and the service you are providing to support them?"

These questions should be something most companies can respond to without further thought. But many companies, even those that have been in business for a number of years, may be hard pressed to provide more than informed guesses when presented with these questions. For companies that have grown quickly and expanded their product lines, the idea that they can still personally know each customer or draw significant inferences from occasional contacts leads to misunderstandings, incorrect perceptions, and serious shortcomings in their efforts to satisfy customers as the customer base and business grows. For even the best companies in today's dynamic markets, keeping a finger on the pulse of the customer is difficult without some proactive and regular approach to collecting and analyzing information about the changing markets and customer base.

The Importance of Systematic and Structured Research

The way to achieve a better understanding of our customers, as well as many other important aspects of the business environment, is through structured research methods. When we think about customers, the people who directly buy our product are usually who we have in mind. We tend to focus on this population in our attempts to educate, inform, and persuade others about the quality of our product and company. In reality, though, companies must be concerned about many different constituencies that can have some influence over the purchase decision and ultimate level of customer satisfaction with the organization's product or service. Besides those "real" customers who actually purchase the products, there are other equally important groups who we have to persuade and who might "buy" our messages and image of the product to, in turn, influence and have impact on the decisions of the actual buying customers. These other groups are all the representatives, agents, contractors, and even internal employees—the people representing an organization who provide support in some way to serve the revenue-generating customer. These additional constituencies are very important to the selling process and should be as much a target for our research as the actual buyer of the product.

No matter which group of "customers" you are looking at, gaining a greater understanding of their attitudes, perceptions of the product, and expectations for it is important. Using a wide variety of structured research methods is the most reliable way to do this. The implication of structure doesn't mean that the research effort needs to be time-consuming and costly. More accurately, structure means that data should be collected in a regular and systematic way, using effective methods that can provide the most appropriate focus on the customer and on other influential groups of interest.

Superior customer service is a matter of meeting customers' needs and exceeding their expectations. To do this, we must know definitively what these requirements are. The purpose of systematic research is to provide solid and unbiased analysis of what these requirements actually comprise. Often, customer needs and expectations are much different from what we *think* they are. Without the benefit of effective research, we would only continue to make wrong assumptions about customers, until the overwhelming negative customer feedback indicated that something was seriously wrong with our original assumptions.

Superior customer service is a matter of meeting customers' needs and exceeding their expectations.

In their book *Service Quality*, the authors Berry, Bennett, and Brown identified four common problems that are the source of most customer service dissatisfactions:[1]

1. The organization's idea of customers' expectations is actually much different from what customers really want.
2. Standards for service that management develop set quality levels that are inadequate to meet customer expectations. So, even though customer needs

are understood, and service providers may do their jobs well in delivering great service, the service is not adequate to meet customers' expectations.

3. What is communicated by the company to the customer is not an accurate representation of what the service standards call for and what the provider actually delivers. As a result, the service delivered is different from what customers expected.

4. The service provider fails in its mission and delivers service that may actually be much different from what was specified, meeting neither the organization's nor the customers' goals.

Three of the four problem areas above relate to how well we understand the customers and what they are expecting from the product. How do we avoid these problems? Rather than second-guessing, we should find out what customers are really looking for before we define strategies and take appropriate action. This principle is the foundation for good customer service represented by the first step in the Service Synergy Model—identifying who your customers are and what they expect from you that would qualify as good customer service.

A Lesson from the Automobile Industry

Automobile manufacturers historically were criticized for the service experience, or lack thereof, which they delivered to their customers. This phenomenon can be traced back to the original Henry Ford marketing strategy to "give the customers any color they want, so long as it's black." Today, automobile manufacturers have moved dramatically away from Ford's original focus, which emphasized production efficiency over customer choice. With the level of competition they face, automobile manufacturers have a greater awareness of the importance of customer satisfaction to continued success in their business. Today, they are as aggressive as any other marketing-intensive organization in seeking customer input on a variety of levels to stay in touch with the purchasers of their products. The recognition of how the entire purchase cycle affects customer retention has led them to evaluate the total experience. Their research starts at the very beginning, when the customer first enters the lot for an initial look at the product, and continues with every decision point in between, including the test-drive, the interaction with salespeople, the leasing or financing experience, and the encounter with the service department. This effort has rewarded those proactive carmakers and their dealers with repeat business, customer loyalty, and valuable word-of-mouth referrals. Conversely, those manufacturers who have failed to stay in touch with their customers have seen demand for their products drop as a result.

My own automobile-shopping experience demonstrates how far manufacturers have come in trying to exceed customer expectations. After purchasing my most recent vehicle, I assumed that once I left the lot I would hear nothing more from the dealer until the next time I was ready to purchase. Instead, I was pleasantly surprised by the number of feedback mechanisms the dealer used to reinforce my original purchase decision, determine my satisfaction level with the process, correct any problems, and ensure my continued loyalty to the brand.

On the day of my purchase, virtually everyone at the dealership I came in contact with personally shook my hand and thanked me for the business. This included the sales manager, other salespeople on the floor, and the office support staff.

By the next day, a call came from the salesperson, inquiring about any problems and whether I was satisfied with the process. Several days later, a similar call came from the sales manager. A few days later, I received a letter from the service manager, asking about any problems and introducing the dealer's service department. Finally, about one week after that, a market-research firm contacted me to take a survey with detailed questions about my satisfaction with the vehicle, the purchase experience, and the dealer.

The dealership obviously was very interested in me as a customer, and in finding out what I liked and disliked about the product and service it provided. Knowing that I will eventually buy another car and will also be likely to tell friends and contacts about my experience, it did its best to identify any problems and to find ways to make any future experience I might have with its people even more positive.

In all, the dealership used eight different methods of feedback, including the focus group I was invited to attend 12 months after I purchased the car, to better understand my level of satisfaction with the product and buying process. Not coincidentally, the latest J. D. Powers market research into brand satisfactions showed this manufacturer ranked near the top in terms of customer satisfaction.

Assumptions about Customer Expectations

Many service initiatives fall short in their design because they make assumptions about customer expectations based on information gathered anecdotally from a limited number of customers, or from only a single source of customer feedback. It is common knowledge within market-polling firms that the context and wording of surveys, the ordering of the questions, and even the time of day the survey is taken can dramatically affect the outcome. The same question asked of the same person at two different times could result in two completely different responses, depending on how the question is asked and who is doing the asking.

Basing an entire service strategy on feedback received from only one method can be risky, because that single approach may not provide a completely accurate view of the customer. Similarly, it is important to continually monitor the needs and satisfaction levels of customers because customer satisfaction is a moving target, with expectations and performance standards continually changing.

Customer satisfaction is a moving target, with expectations and performance standards continually changing.

Many methods can be used to identify customer needs. Incorporating a range of varied research techniques into your planning process will provide a more comprehensive and accurate picture of customers. Alternative methods that approach the same concepts from a slightly different perspective, to get a more rounded response from customers, can be used to further validate or elaborate on the results of other research.

Asking managers about the methods they use to gather information for better understanding of their customers yields a variety of answers. One of the most frequently cited methods for determining customer satisfaction is monitoring the number of complaint calls customers place. Although this type of tracking has its uses, the technique applied in isolation is an example of how limited approaches can unintentionally lead to invalid or incomplete information and wrong conclusions about customers. The reasons for this are obvious.

First, unless a formalized complaint-tracking and -analysis system is in place to help categorize the nature of the complaints, look for trends, and compare against historical performance, the measure of complaint volume alone does not provide much useful information about customer satisfaction.

Second, even with this type of system in place, the measure of complaints provides an incomplete picture of the customer-service satisfaction level across the universe of customers you may be interested in. As discussed in chapter 1, it is common that most customers will not complain until their level of dissatisfaction becomes quite high. This means that you won't hear from the majority of your unhappy customers until they are already extremely dissatisfied, and not before. This problem makes the technique of using customer-complaint calls an after-the-fact, or reactive, measure of customer satisfaction level. Any information that the process finally yields may come too late to take corrective action.

The importance of tracking complaint levels should in no way be minimized; but wouldn't it be better to avoid those complaints entirely by identifying up-front what is most important to customers, and acting to deliver products and services that satisfy those expectations? To do that successfully requires effective use of research methods that can help us understand who our customers are and what they need from us, all in a dynamic and timely manner. These research methods, when applied appropriately, not only give us useful information about customers in general, but also often can help to identify potential service issues with existing customers, including those who don't complain, while there is still time to take corrective action. Getting this feedback sooner rather than later also allows modification of the underlying strategies that would continue to cause problems with new customers if those problems are not corrected.

Effective Research Methods to Understand Customer Needs

Although an organization with a dedicated budget may choose to hire professional market-research firms for customized and continuous customer analysis, many less costly and even free approaches are available that companies can take advantage of to better understand their customers. Some of these options are listed in the following sections.

Published Sources

A wealth of existing information is available about customer service. A walk through any library or bookstore reveals hundreds of books that have been pub-

I recently experienced an example of this quality-assurance-monitoring program after I had taken my second car in for repairs. A few days after I got the car back, I was irritated to notice some small dents that appeared to have been made by the mechanic during the repair process. Because this was an older car, and the damage was barely noticeable, I determined that it wasn't worth the hassle to argue with the dealer over fault, and I decided not to pursue the situation further. I also decided at the same time, however, that I wouldn't use that dealer again, nor would I purchase my next car there. Before I had a chance to give this much further thought, I received a follow-up call inquiring about my satisfaction with the overall service. After I had explained my situation, I received an immediate call from the service manager with an offer to immediately correct the cosmetic damage, which the shop subsequently did. This follow-up service impressed me greatly and dramatically shifted my previous impression to a much more favorable opinion of the company's service and product.

lished on this topic. In addition to the commercial books, researchers at colleges and universities across the nation have undertaken extensive studies on the art of customer service, all of which have been published in academic journals and leading business magazines. These publications, including *Journal of Marketing, Journal of Marketing Research,* and *Harvard Business Review,* are a good source of information for defining general service strategies and guidelines.

The risk in relying too heavily on this type of information is that it may be too general, out of date, or not relevant to the unique needs of your customers. The University of Michigan Business School, which developed the American Consumer Satisfaction Index in 1994, follows general consumer-satisfaction trends with quarterly updates and provides benchmarking information for companies, professional associations, and government agencies.

Industry and Trade Association Research

As a service to their members, many industry and trade associations undertake research that is industry-specific and readily accessible. The National Association of Home Builders (NAHB) is recognized as the premier authority for those who are part of the homebuilding industry. A visitor to the NAHB website at www.nahb.org will find up-to-date economic and housing data, construction statistics, state and local information, economic-impact reports, housing forecasts, and other relevant information specifically for the homebuilding industry. This research has been compiled into a library of data that is useful for understanding customer behavior more specific to your customers and business than the general sources noted above.

Another industry association, the National Association of Realtors®, has established Real Estate Research Centers around the United States for the specific purpose of studying real-estate issues and trends. Developed in conjunction with public and private universities as well as independent organizations, the locations of these research centers, along with various research reports, can be found at www.realtor.org.

Analyzing Existing Customer, Sales, and Contact Information

Most companies have a treasure trove of information already available through records and databases for existing customers, potential customer contacts, historical sales data, and customer-service logs. Although the information may already exist for your company if you maintain these types of databases, it is usually not presented in a useful summary form that shows meaningful relationships and trends. The process known as *data mining* is a way to better analyze this data to identify those relationships and help to more fully understand the customers who have been contacting you about the product. This type of analysis can help to get additional information from your own company's sales records, market studies, and competitor data, to lend insight into why customers did or did not purchase from you. Figure 4-1 shows some of the companies that provide data-mining software and services.

Observational Research

Another exploratory research method to consider involves personal observation in various situations. For example, managers might spend time visiting new-home sales offices or design centers and listen to how customers talk about the different aspects of their service experience. You might even visit competitors' facilities to observe how they deliver service, along with their customers' reactions

Figure 4-1 Popular Data-Mining Software

Following are selected suppliers of software that provide data-mining capability. These products would normally be used with your existing databases to analyze relationships and develop trends from this information that can help you to better understand your customers. This listing is for reference only and is not meant as an endorsement of these products.

IBM Intelligent Miner for Data
Provides latest data-mining technology and supports full range of mining processes, from data preparation to mining presentation.
www3.ibm.com/software/data/iminer/fordata

Crystal Reports
Crystal Reports supports basic data-trend analysis to explore trends, compare information, and view points of interest in your organization's data using guided workflows.
www.crystaldecisions.com

Microsoft SQL Server 2000
SQL Server 2000 supports data mining with decision trees, clustering, and third-party algorithms for analyzing information from existing databases.
www.microsoft.com/SQL/evaluation/features/datamine.asp

Oracle9i Data Mining
Oracle9i Data Mining, an option to Oracle9i Enterprise Edition, is used for making classifications, predictions, and associations using your existing databases.
www.otn.oracle.com/products/bi/9idmining.html

Salford Systems CART®
A data-mining tool that automatically sifts large, complex databases, searching for and isolating significant patterns and relationships.
www.salford-systems.com

to that service. These observational steps might suggest some new and interesting ideas to consider for your own company.

Casual Interviewing

Customer-service researchers can talk to various people—sales assistants, lenders, design-center representatives, construction supervisors, or even other builders—about the entire service cycle, obtaining their impression of the various steps. They can do this by striking up a conversation rather than acting as interviewers. The ad-hoc nature of this approach can result in obtaining more insights from the customer than structured surveys offer, but its subjective character makes it highly dependent on personal interpretation. For this reason, this technique is normally useful to supplement or reinforce the findings from other more rigorous research methods, rather than as a primary research method.

Point-of-Service Feedback

The most natural time to ask for feedback on the service is at the point of delivery. Whenever anyone provides some part of the core service, a natural complement to the service should be to find out how well the customer is satisfied with the service provided, before the provider and customer conclude the service activity. For example, after I had completed the purchase negotiation on an automobile, the salesperson asked for feedback on the sales process. Before I left the dealership, I was asked to fill out a simple five-question comment card and hand it to the receptionist. At that point, my impressions, whether negative or positive, were still fresh and at the top of my mind.

Asking for feedback so quickly helps to immediately identify any service problems and determine how well expectations were met. This feedback allows management to take any corrective action or provide necessary coaching right away. Additionally, if the salesperson did an exemplary job, that, too, can be recognized and reinforced just as quickly. The more time that lapses between the service delivery and the positive recognition, the less meaningful the recognition becomes to the recipient, losing value as a motivator.

Customer Training Sessions

Information gained from customer training sessions is another source often overlooked for customer input. Training customers on proper use of your products is itself a big help in avoiding service problems, but the two-way and detailed communication about the product that takes place during such training is also a great method for better understanding what customers are expecting from the product and the service provider. Statistics have shown that up to 40 percent of customer complaints result from customer misuse or unrealistic expectations about the product.[2] If customers are not shown how to properly use the products or services they have purchased, the service provider will be blamed for any dissatisfaction the customer experiences.

For example, my automobile manufacturer wanted to be sure I knew how to operate all the features that came with the vehicle. Before I left the dealership, a video and CD that demonstrated every aspect of the vehicle's operation were given to me. For most service providers with smaller customer bases, incurring the relatively high production costs associated with these types of media is not necessary. Instead, stand-up training programs or short, one-on-one coaching sessions may be a more cost-effective and personalized way to accomplish the same objective.

Focus-Group Interviewing

Another way of gathering important customer information—and one that is used all too infrequently—is the *focus group*. A focus group is a somewhat informal research group consisting of 6 to 10 people who are current or likely users of your product or service. They may be existing customers, interested parties, or completely anonymous groups selected by some predetermined criteria with explicit objectives in mind. These people are invited to gather for a few hours to discuss a specific topic. A trained facilitator questions group members about their feelings and behavior toward your service delivery, and encourages as much free-flowing discussion as possible. The comments are recorded, and the answers provide a basis for more formalized survey construction.

Besides the research value, the focus group can serve as a valuable public-relations tool because people are always flattered when someone asks for their opinion. Depending on the objective and attendees, focus groups can be conducted in several ways:

1. With complete objectivity, conducted by a third-party facilitator who then reports back to you.
2. With you as an anonymous observer, sometimes watching and listening through a one-way mirror, to get full benefit of the personal expressions and body language as the group is interviewed.
3. In two segments, with the opening session as above, in which the attendees first have no knowledge of your company's involvement. In the following segment, you and your company will be introduced, which allows for interactive dialogue directly with the members of the focus group, who are now fully aware of who is sponsoring the research.

Focus groups are especially useful for gathering more detailed user information of a subjective nature because they can elicit from users spontaneous and sometimes surprising ideas that were not anticipated prior to the research.

Formal Customized Research

Not content to fully rely on customer contacts at the point of sale, the car dealership in the earlier scenario employed an outside research firm to conduct additional research on my service experience. Professional survey companies have expertise in survey design, collection techniques, and results interpretation. Their findings are highly reliable because of their expertise and investment in hardware and software infrastructure, which allows information to be gathered and compiled in the most efficient and unbiased manner.

STRATEGIES FOR CONDUCTING A FOCUS GROUP[3]

The focus group should be assembled by inviting six to nine customers or people who are interested in the product to the two-hour session. Several separate sessions should be planned, to get a more representative group sample and eliminate individual biases from a few strong personalities. Depending on the objectives, the group may be advised that your company is the sponsor, or this fact may be withheld to keep the discussion more generic. Objectives and suitable questions should be determined and a general script prepared that the moderator can follow. Following is an example of the direction this discussion can take for the home builder's audience:

1. Pose a question to the focus group in such a way that it will encourage a list of customer expectations. Questions might include the following:
   a. *What are your expectations of the home builder's representatives during the home-purchase process?*
   b. *When you are shopping for a new home, what would make the experience an excellent one for you?*
   c. *What does it take for a service provider to impress you?*
2. Ask participants to write down as many responses as they can.
3. When all have had time to think of their responses, ask the participants to share them with the other members of the focus group. Have a colleague record all responses.
4. Once all responses have been recorded, ask the group to refine the list by eliminating redundancies and clarifying any ideas that require further explanation.
5. As a group, have participants prioritize the list of expectations in order of importance to the customer.
6. Finally, have the group rate and evaluate different service providers, yours included, on how well the identified expectations are being met.

Following the session, an analysis consisting of anything from a summary narrative with overview of the findings, to a more detailed report that quantitatively analyzes responses, and any significant supporting or particularly insightful quotes from the participants, should be prepared. If recorded, a transcript may be prepared so that the actual responses can be reviewed again, if needed, for clarification.

Eliant (formerly National Survey Systems), in Irvine, California, is the largest consumer-research company in the country that caters exclusively to the building industry. Each year, Eliant conducts more than 200,000 home-buyer surveys to help builders exceed the expectations of their customers. In addition to the services he provides to individual builder clients, Bob Mirman, Eliant's founder and CEO, shares industry best practices, general research results, and techniques for increasing customer satisfaction ratings at the company's website, www.eliant.com.

Customer Hotlines

Wanting to make sure they were on top of any issues that might surface while we owned the car, our dealership strategically placed fluorescent stickers containing a customer-hotline number on our paperwork and on various parts of the automobile. Should we ever have any questions or concerns, these reminders encourage contact with the dealership. Customer hotlines provide a central, toll-free number by which all calls are filtered, making it easy for the customer to contact the manufacturer or dealer.

When customers know that they can make relatively little effort to get some kind of response, they are much more willing to take action than if they have to hunt through owner's manuals long ago tucked into drawers or files, dig out old business cards, or search through the telephone book and call several different numbers as they try to get resolution to a problem. Another important benefit of the hotline is that it provides a higher-level contact for customers, offering them an alternate avenue for problem resolution when they might feel that the original service provider has not been responsive. For the manufacturer, hotline calls provide a useful indicator of the satisfaction level its dealers or other independent service representatives are achieving.

The open communication channel the hotline provides means that the company can receive regular and immediate information regarding issues, such as product failures, that might indicate some ongoing quality problem that could affect other customers. This allows the organization to be proactive in communicating these issues so that existing customers can avoid similar problems. When companies can provide proactive interference and alert customers to potential problems before they occur, they will be seen as exceeding their customers' expectations and will come one step closer to earning the trust and loyalty of those customers.

Any company that makes the effort to install a customer hotline should make sure it can also take full advantage of this communications tools by putting in place a system for recording any issues that are brought forward. Keeping track of the nature of calls to a customer hotline shows the type and frequency of problems most important to your customers. A tracking form, such as the call sheet shown in Figure 4-2, is one way to document such calls. Only through quantifiable information can the service provider monitor performance and identify important trends to better understand the customer expectations.

Web-Based Research and Data Collection

The Internet has added a dramatic new dimension to research for understanding customers. The Web has made it possible to do relatively low-cost and powerful searches to access a wealth of readily available information from sources around the globe. A company's own website also provides a great opportunity to gain insights on potential customers who visit the site, as well as to generate actual leads for future sales. A properly constructed website will allow casual visitors to access general information anonymously, but it will also move them to a registration form and limited survey questions once they have self-qualified by

Figure 4-2 Call Sheet

NAME _____

ADDRESS: _____

CITY, STATE, ZIP: _____

TELEPHONE (Work): _____ (Home): _____ (Mobile): _____

Description of Request:

_____

_____

_____

Expected Results:

_____

_____

_____

OFFICIAL USE ONLY

Date: _____

Time Received: _____

Person Taking Request: _____

Action Taken: _____

_____

_____

FOLLOW-UP

Date: _____ Time: _____ By: _____

Actual Result: _____

_____

How satisfied was the customer with the service and ultimate resolution? Circle one.

High Dissatisfaction Did not meet needs or expectations	Low Dissatisfaction Met needs, but did not meet expectations	Low Satisfaction Met needs and met expectations	High Satisfaction Met needs and exceeded expectations
1	2	3	4

clicking through to request more detailed information, obtain product brochures, or be contacted by a sales representative. After a database of qualified visitors to the website has been developed, the company can use this database as a regular communication vehicle or for periodic "instant" surveys of specific issues. See Figure 4-3 for a typical example of such a survey. For basic research that involves only a few issues, an inexpensive way to get benefits similar to that of the focus group described above is to rely on these Internet or e-mail surveys, as well as discussion forums. For monitoring Internet activity, many tools, services, and commercial products are available to help businesses readily "data mine" visitor information.

Research Implications for the Builder

The building industry is highly competitive. Most builders are actively engaged in multiple research efforts to better understand what their customers want in a final product and help differentiate against competitors. It is common to see builders use many of these research methods before the architectural design phase of the community to better understand the design, style, floor plan, and other option and amenity preferences of their target markets. Extensive research also has been conducted by the National Association of Home Builders regarding demographic and economic trends of the new home-buying public. However, the component often missed in this type of research is service delivery ratings of all service providers who play a role in delivering the builder's product to the ultimate user.

Professional research firms spend thousands of hours polling home buyers about their experiences. These research specialists can provide cumulative data and draw general inferences about service delivery that serves as useful guidelines. The service-oriented builder should begin with research into customer preferences and subsequently use those results to establish benchmark standards of service delivery for all personnel involved in critical contacts with customers. This includes the sales, title, lender, design, and customer-service representatives. After those standards are in place, the builder is ready to monitor the impact of the service delivery on customers and use the quantifiable data to make any necessary corrections to ensure that service delivery enhances the product itself.

A. James Grant once said, "There are two large groups of people in the world—those who start well and finish poorly, and those who start poorly and finish well."[4] Without adequate research, builders have no idea where they are starting. Because the finish is more important than the start and is the only true indicator of how well builders meet their customers' needs, think of research as the insurance policy for keeping on target and guarding against any missteps. All the research methods presented here can be applied effectively to gain a better understanding of customers.

Figure 4-3 Sample Internet-Based Survey

Question 1

What do you like best about your new home?

_____ Lot size

_____ Lot location

_____ Floor plan

_____ General community appearance

_____ Proximity to schools

_____ Near by shopping areas

Question 2 (Answer Required)

Would you refer family and friends to one of our communities?

_____ No

_____ Yes

Question 3

How would you rate the installation and workmanship of the following:

	Poor				Excellent
Air Conditioning	1	2	3	4	5
Appliances	1	2	3	4	5
Cabinets	1	2	3	4	5
Doors	1	2	3	4	5
Fireplace	1	2	3	4	5
Heating	1	2	3	4	5
Light Switches	1	2	3	4	5
Outlets	1	2	3	4	5

(continued)

Figure 4-3 Continued

Question 4

On a scale of 1 to 10 with 10 being the best, how would you rate the quality of your home?

1	2	3	4	5	6	7	8	9	10

____   ____   ____   ____   ____   ____   ____   ____   ____   ____

This ends the closed-questions section. Below you will find two open-ended questions.

Question 5

Would you be interested in participating in future consumer focus groups or opinion surveys? If so, please provide your e-mail address or telephone number below.

Question 6

Please fill out your final remarks or questions below. If you want a response, please add your name and e-mail address or telephone number.

Submit

Summary

To simply assume we know what customers want is not enough in today's competitive environment. We must have in-depth information about who our customers are and what they expect from our product and services. Using organized research methods together with effective analysis of data collected from this research is the best way to build a clear picture of our customers, to develop effective service strategies. A double benefit is obtained from some research methods, such as follow-up surveys like the example in Figure 4-4, because they can provide an opportunity to both gather information about customers and also identify and take immediate corrective action for any issues customers have that are causing dissatisfaction. A wide range of research methods is available to the manager for gathering information. Appropriate use of these methods for developing initial strategy, and for continuous monitoring of results, will help an organization to more effectively provide good customer service.

Figure 4-4 Follow-Up Survey

Please rate your satisfaction with our service.

	Strongly Agree	Agree	No Opinion	Disagree	Strongly Disagree
Your request was handled professionally.	❏	❏	❏	❏	❏
Our representatives were friendly and courteous.	❏	❏	❏	❏	❏
Your request was handled within the given time frame.	❏	❏	❏	❏	❏
Our representatives were helpful in answering questions.	❏	❏	❏	❏	❏
Our representatives took the extra effort to serve you well.	❏	❏	❏	❏	❏

What, if anything, could we do to improve the service we provide?

OPTIONAL:

Name: _____   Phone: _____

Address: _____

City: _____   State: _____   Zip: _____

SERVICE ASSESSMENT

1. Why is research essential for good customer service?
2. Identify the number of methods your organization or department uses to obtain information about your customers. How much of this research relates to customer-service needs?
3. Select one research method discussed in this chapter that is currently not used by your organization. Create a plan for gathering information about the service preferences of your customer base. Prepare a summary of your findings.

Setting Service Standards

Introduction

I recently decided to take up the game of golf. Although golf is a difficult and somewhat complex game to learn, the objective is simple: Get the ball in the cup, taking as few shots as possible. After an initial learning period, I am now starting to experience the thrill of hitting a long, straight drive that soars through the air and lands close to the intended target. If I consistently accomplish this objective on every hole, I can expect to finish the round with a relatively decent score.

Now the term "relatively decent score" is somewhat subjective. What is acceptable to me may not be at all reasonable for a colleague whose scores are normally much better than mine. Additionally, every golf course is different, with different characteristics and degrees of difficulty, so a good score on one course may represent something completely different on another. The rules of the game acknowledge this problem and provide a set of standards that afford a more objective measure of each player's performance. This performance measure is *par,* which refers to the number of strokes typically required to get the ball from the tee into the cup. This value varies for each hole and golf course, depending on the terrain, natural or manmade hazards, and other factors unique to the course. In essence, the par measure is a reference standard to indicate how well each player is performing in that unique situation as he or she follows the established course and guidelines for play.

Importance of Standards for Quality Service

The game of golf has standards for player conduct and performance on each golf course. These standards are intended to make the experience more consistent and satisfying for players. A company must similarly identify the operating standards and performance measures that will show its employees how they should deliver service, to consistently satisfy customers and achieve the desired objectives of the organization.

Like par in golf, the idea of standards is simple in concept, but more difficult in practice to implement because of the many variables that result from the person-to-person interaction of customers with various service providers. Service standards go beyond mere service guidelines or task descriptions. Although specific guidelines or task descriptions may be appropriate to include as part of some service standards, the main purpose of the standards is to define specific outcomes and accomplishments from the service effort. These outcomes and accomplishments achieve the customer-satisfaction levels that fulfill the organization's objectives. To define different levels of performance is useful as a measurement reference, but, as you know from our earlier discussion about customer expectations, to strive for only minimum or average levels of customer satisfaction would not typically be a desirable goal for a successful customer-service function. Instead, we must go beyond customers' basic expectations to achieve high levels of satisfaction that are beneficial to the customer and that meet the organization's objectives: retaining repeat customers, increasing referral rates, and expanding sales.

Goals that are specific, challenging, and continually monitored through regular feedback serve as a potent motivating force that leads to higher performance.

Various researchers' conclusions about the benefits of goal setting have been unanimous on one important point: The simple act of clearly defining goals in written form can significantly increase the likelihood of success in achieving these goals. Goals that are specific, challenging, and continually monitored through regular feedback serve as a potent motivating force that leads to higher performance.[1]

Telling employees their goal is something such as "You are expected to deliver the best quality customer service" is an admirable suggestion, but this goal is too ambiguous to be of any use either as a motivator or a measure of performance. The result would be as many variations of this ambiguous goal as there are employees and varying experience levels. Managers can convey a clear and unambiguous picture of expectations to employees only by defining precise service goals. A *service goal* is a measurable desired result, or level of customer service, toward which everyone in the organization is working. Well-defined service standards, which are the means for achieving the goals, allow service providers, and especially new employees, to know how they are to behave on the job; help them to assimilate better into the organization; and allow them to perform at their highest levels of productivity much more quickly.

Written service goals are an important communication tool for both managers and employees. Too often, managers assume their expectations are so obvious that no alternate interpretation is possible, so putting them in writing is unnecessary. This type of thinking quickly leads to unsatisfactory service and inconsistent performance throughout the organization. With written standards, managers and employees together have a useful benchmark for measuring performance.

Standards must be predicated on knowing the characteristics of your customers and user groups, and what they expect from you. But making the effort to understand the needs and expectations of your customers will be of little value unless you also understand how to act appropriately on this information. These measurable standards, when clearly defined in written form, will establish the appropriate behavior of all those who might be involved in the customer interaction, whether they are internal employees or external vendors who play a role in the product or service delivery. Time and time again, it is proven that the companies most successful in delivering outstanding customer service are the same ones who have established, and constantly strive to achieve, measurable goals for providing quality service.

As with any set of goals, customer-service standards are best when clearly stated and defined with *measurable* outcomes. The service standards should be defined for each department, vendor, and trade contractor who has a role, either directly or indirectly, in providing service to customers.

Effective customer-service standards need to focus on two categories of requirements. The first category is quality standards for delivery of the basic product or service itself—what is necessary to meet customer needs, including those functions, features, and performance issues that have been previously specified. The second category includes guidelines and goals for satisfying customer expectations in those areas that go beyond the basic product specifications and relate more to the service-delivery process and interactions with the customer. Figure 5-1 illustrates these two categories, along with the types of issues that each includes.

The actions required to satisfy basic needs becomes the minimum acceptable customer-service standard. There is an inherent danger in consistently performing at or below the minimum, because this level does not result in customer satisfaction to a degree that builds customer loyalty. Alternatively, establishing standards that are so high that they cannot reasonably be achieved creates

---

EXAMPLES OF SAMPLE SERVICE GOALS

- To achieve an average 95 percent rating on all returned customer-satisfaction surveys for the current fiscal year.
- To reduce the number of repeat warranty calls by 50 percent from the previous fiscal year.
- To respond to service requests within four hours.

Figure 5-1 Categories of Service Standards

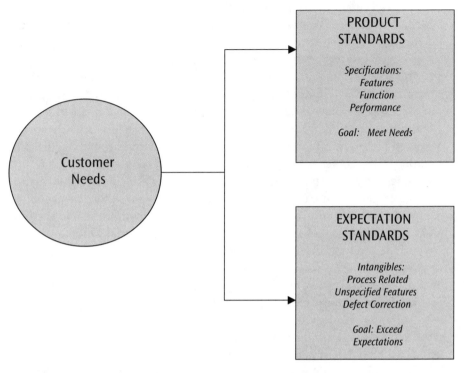

unreal expectations for customers and sets up the service provider for failure that can be nearly as damaging as setting standards that are too low.

Consider this example. Suppose a customer calls at 8:00 A.M. with an urgent service request. If the standard for response time is two hours maximum, the dispatcher may inform the customer that someone will be there by 10:00 A.M. If the service provider arrives early, at 9:30 A.M., the customer's expectations are exceeded. However, if an overly zealous dispatcher instead promises a technician at the premises in one hour, the expectations of the customer have been altered, and the same 9:30 A.M. arrival may now result in reduced customer-satisfaction levels.

Standards are such a critical component of the service process because they not only guide employees, but they also are the first step in managing customers' expectations, which are key to the overall perception of service quality. Ideally, standards should be established that clearly define minimum acceptable performance levels, but the company culture and reward system reinforcing these levels of performance should be structured to encourage staff to perform at levels that continually exceed these minimum standards.

Setting Service Standards

How do managers go about setting suitable service standards for activities under their control? The establishment of service standards is the next major step on the Service Synergy Model for creating an effective service culture. The exercise of developing service standards builds on the corporate vision defined by management, combined with the understanding of customer characteristics and needs that have been developed through effective research methods.

The corporate vision for a service culture should define general strategies and a philosophy for the customer-service function. The actual standards break down the customer-service strategies into better defined and measurable components, with details unique to the specific service activities. Knowing who the customers are and what those customers want allows measurable standards to be defined that will guide the appropriate behavior of all those who might be involved in providing for these customer needs. To better understand what should be included in these standards, we can look to available research that shows which factors customers consider to be most important for quality service.

Researchers at Texas A & M University were at the forefront of defining quality service in the mid-1980s. They conducted focus-group sessions with customers and in-depth interviews with executives in an attempt to develop a model of service quality. Their exploratory research revealed that consumers use a core set of parameters when they are evaluating their service experiences. Figure 5-2 shows the 10 key categories that emerged from these focus-group studies.[2] Service standards should always be based on analysis of the specific customer situation, but managers can use these initial 10 dimensions as a starting point for identifying their customers' priorities, and then set service standards for their departments and vendors accordingly.

Beyond the general categories of service needs identified by this study, there also are considerations unique to each of the different service experiences. These service opportunities, or critical contact points, at which customers may encounter the need for service, can involve different service providers and may have customer expectations that are outside the norm. The best way to define service standards that provide for both general and unique customer needs is to identify and analyze these critical contact points. From there, standards are developed that include both the general and the specific requirements that arise in these different opportunities for service interaction. Setting service goals that are specific, measurable, and timely will provide a way of measuring employee or vendor progress toward attaining these goals, and of ensuring consistency of delivery.

Notice how the following two examples differ. The first leaves room for service failures, depending on how quickly the follow-up is made. The second leaves little room for error.

1. Representatives will keep purchasers advised of construction progress during the purchase period.
2. Representatives will contact all purchasers via e-mail or telephone once a week to update them on the construction activities that are taking place that week.

The first example tells staff representatives what they must do to ensure exceptional service delivery. However, the method and frequency of contact are not

Figure 5-2 10 Dimensions of Quality Service

DIMENSION	DESCRIPTION
1. ACCESSIBILITY	Making contact easy for customers without going through long voice-mail loops or waiting on hold for long periods of time to request or receive service. Refers to hours of operation, location of community, ease of finding it, or timely approach upon entering a model community.
2. COMMUNICATION	Keeping customers informed about the status of their purchase or work requests. Information is conveyed in a language customers can understand. Refers to the use of real-estate jargon and unfamiliar legal, financing, or escrow terminology.
3. COMPETENCE	Possessing the required skills and knowledge to perform the needed function. Refers to the ability to complete contracts and financing-qualification forms in a thorough and accurate manner, and to explain legal, finance, title, and escrow processes to the customer.
4. COURTESY	Demonstrating politeness, respect, consideration, and friendliness to all customers. Refers to verbal communications and nonverbal body language. Also refers to consideration for customer's property, schedule, and other pre- and post-purchase activities.
5. CREDIBILITY	Putting customers' best interests as the highest priority. Refers to honesty, integrity, and trustworthiness in all aspects of the home purchase.
6. RELIABILITY	Performing the service right the first time, and consistently honoring commitments. Refers to the ability to eliminate callbacks on service requests and to follow-through on promises made.
7. RESPONSIVENESS	Conveying a willingness to provide service in a timely and prompt manner. Refers to response times on any type of service request, from faxing necessary documents, to completing paperwork, to repair requests.
8. SECURITY	Maintaining the safety and security of the environment. Refers to maintaining a safe physical environment, and the confidentiality of information with which service providers have been entrusted.
9. TANGIBLES	Maintaining the appearance of physical facilities, the service personnel, and any other physical representations of the service provider. Can refer to the appearance of the community, uniforms worn by service personnel, tools or equipment used when providing service, marketing materials, contracts, and any other physical representations.
10. UNDERSTANDING THE CUSTOMER	Making the effort to understand the unique needs of individual customers. Can refer to learning about special familial requirements, recognizing customers by name, and knowing how customers want the home-purchase process handled.

spelled out clearly. One person could meet the standard by making contact once or twice throughout the construction period. That amount of contact will probably not be sufficient enough to exceed the customer's expectations.

The second example is much more specific, pointing out both the method and frequency of contact throughout the construction period. The information communicated will vary from week to week, depending on the activities that took place. The relatively small cost and time investment will reap much greater rewards for the representatives and the company in the form of high customer-satisfaction levels, and potential referral business.

Every organization should have clear, written "standards of excellence" that are established and maintained for all customer interactions—both internal and external. Figure 5-3 provides a reality check to determine whether your standards are written in such a way that they leave no room for interpretation or misunderstanding by those charged with service delivery. All in all, these standards represent what customers expect from us and what we have a right to expect of one another. By establishing clear, concise, observable, and realistic standards, we define precisely what we want our service image to be. The standards become the reference point at which quality customer service begins.

Implications for the Builder in Setting Service Standards

Founded in 1984, Eliant (formerly known as National Survey Systems) has conducted extensive research on new home buyers, using focus groups and buyer surveys. This research has shown that, for the builder community, simply satisfying customers does little to distinguish builders from their competitors. Instead, overall service that exceeds home buyers' expectations is necessary to make enough of an impression that fervent endorsements, referrals, and repeat buying results.[3] This information in an indication to home builders that they should clearly define standards, to encourage service representatives to continually exceed expectations.

Eliant findings on key home-buyer-satisfaction factors closely mirror those identified by the Texas A & M researchers. This means that the 10 key general categories identified by the Texas A & M researchers are consistent with those of, and important to, home buyers. So these categories should be a primary reference for builders as they establish service standards.

In the category of communication, Eliant found that the builders whose employees and representatives were proactive in communicating during the purchase-closing process received much higher satisfaction rankings than builders whose personnel did not. This suggests that standards should be developed that accomplish goals such as the following:

- Encourage salespeople to be proactive in keeping the buyer informed of construction progress.

Figure 5-3 Do Your Standards Meet the Test?

Answer the following questions for each standard that you write. If you can answer Yes for each one, then your standard will be easily understood by others.		
Is the standard clear, concise, and specific; not general?	Yes	No
Is the standard described in such a way that it can be measured?	Yes	No
Does the standard define specific performance behavior?	Yes	No
Is the standard aimed high, but still attainable?	Yes	No
Does the standard include a deadline or time interval for completion?	Yes	No

- Require the lender to communicate loan status information regularly to the customer.
- Direct the customer-service department to give the customer timely information about the status of repair requests.

In contrast, in the area of responsiveness, the research found that customers who were forced to use a mail-in request ranked their builders much lower than those builders who provided immediate acknowledgements to their customers. This doesn't mean that builders shouldn't use technology to communicate with customers. Customers weren't looking for immediate resolution; they were simply looking for a timely acknowledgement, something that a telephone call provided but an e-mail did not. A service standard considering this finding might look like this:[4]

> Within 30 minutes of receiving a request for repairs, customer-service representatives will call to inform the customer of the date and time when the requested service will be scheduled.

Clearly, this is an area in which the builder should consider setting specific service standards, because it's one of the main characteristics that differentiates the best builders from their competitors. Sample service standards that relate to responsiveness are included in Figure 5-4. Remember, though, that standards should be based on the needs of your specific customer groups. Although some standards can apply across organizational and departmental boundaries, customer needs at points of critical contact should ultimately dictate the true standards for service.

Builders have to deal with the unusual situation in which many of the service providers representing the product are independent representatives who are, for the most part, outside of the builders' day-to-day control. Figure 5-5 illustrates the interaction of several of the different groups involved in providing good customer service for builders' customers. With the builders' products at the center of the experience, other service groups, as represented, play an integral role in the service effort by making their own individual contributions at critical contacts with customers. Although each group has responsibility for

Figure 5-4 Sample Service Standards

1. All voice-mail messages and inquiries will be returned within two hours of receiving them. If you do not know the answer, let the caller know you are attempting to obtain the information.

2. Vendors and trade contractors who perform warranty service will contact the builder's customer-service department, relaying the status of the work order within 15 minutes of leaving the customer's property.

3. Vendors and trade contractors will demonstrate respect for the customer's property by wearing foot covers over boots or shoes while performing service in the home's interior.

4. Lenders will provide a weekly report to home buyers, via e-mail or telephone conversation, updating them on the status of their loan.

5. Telephones will be answered by the second ring. When you are away from your desk, calls will be forwarded to voice mail to prevent callers from hearing more than two rings.

Figure 5-5 Creating Seamless Service Delivery

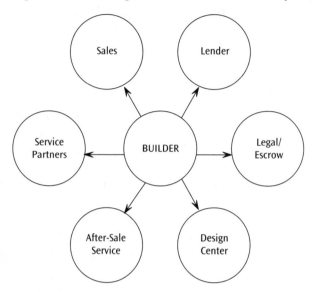

establishing and maintaining its own service standards, these standards also must be consistent with those of the respective builders. When service partners are not directly controlled by builders, the builders need to exercise particular care to ensure that partner standards are closely matched with their own. This is one reason that selection of the various trade contractors should also include a screening of builders' customer-service strategies, procedures, and standards. When partner cultures don't fit well with builders' established service culture, these partners can easily become the weak links in the chain for providing good customer service, by contradicting builders' established performance standards.

A survey on construction quality conducted by Eliant showed that some categories of construction receive consistently lower buyer-satisfaction ratings across virtually all areas of the country.[5] Those categories receiving the lowest scores include landscaping, paint, HVAC, flooring, plumbing, and doors. Coincidentally, these are all areas that trade contractors or outside vendors usually service.

Given the consistently low buyer ratings of these categories, builders can be assured that there will be definite callbacks to the home after the move-in as a result of these problem areas unless the builders take some action to establish and enforce more consistent standards with those contractors. Compounding the problem is the fact that these groups are most likely to be some of the last to have contact with customers, at the final stages of the construction process. The risk in this situation is that the last impression customers receive of builders is from those trade contractors who may have the weakest performance in satisfying customers' expectations. This impact is not something builders want to leave to chance. Instead, they need to exercise a greater degree of control over the interactions between these trade contractors and customers by ensuring that acceptable service standards are in place for these and all other vendors who come into contact with customers. To address this problem, many builders have already designed their own standards for trade contractors, and they require a commitment that the trade contractors will adhere to these standards before they award trade-contractor contracts. Look at Figure 5-6 to see a sample standards agreement.

Getting Started

Creating service standards will take a significant effort initially, but the long-term payoff is worth the investment. Customers, both internal and external, maintain their own barometers of how service provided at critical contact points affects them. By listening to your customers, you can create a summary of expectations that will provide a valuable roadmap for establishing service standards within your organization. In establishing standards, it is important to remember that they apply to everyone in the organization, not just sales representatives or those who have contact with the buying public. Standards should include all job functions and support services. The best way to start setting standards is by analyzing each critical contact point on the homebuyer's decision track. By discussing what customers expect and what detracts from their experience, you can create the framework for writing meaningful service standards. Figure 5-7 is an example of how to analyze one of the builder's critical contact points—in this case, a homebuyer's initial contact with the customer-service department, to request service.

To close, here are some last guidelines for builders to help in setting quality service standards:

- Begin by examining current service practices at critical contact points. What is happening that causes frustrations for customers? In this case, formal market research and data analysis, with constant monitoring of customer feedback, can be very helpful.
- Don't operate in a vacuum. Formal research can begin with a simple three-question survey: (1) What did you like most about the new-home purchase process? (2) What did you like least about the new-home purchase process? (3) What improvements would you suggest?
- Draw on the recommendations of employees who have significant experience in the industry. Successful employees have succeeded because they know how to do their job and have been serving the buying public well.
- If your company has a dedicated customer-service department, ask individuals who work there what they think are the most important aspects of service, based on what they hear during the course of their jobs. The answers may be surprising. Compile all the responses into one list, which can become the foundation for establishing standards.
- Ask each person in the company to write "Standards of Excellence" for his or her own job description, using the "10 Service Dimensions" as a guide. Compare these written standards with primary research that has already been done in the building industry, to ensure that the standards are consistent with what new-home purchasers want.

Figure 5-6 Sample Standards Agreement

GENERAL PHILOSOPHY:

Our reputation as one of the leaders in the building industry has been built on our attitude of customer service. To maintain this reputation, each member of our staff and all service partners who meet or provide service on behalf of a customer, whether an employee, vendor, or trade contractor, must adhere to the same standards of service delivery in order to provide a seamless experience for the customer. These standards and expectations are provided to ensure that our goal of courtesy and outstanding service is achieved.

APPEARANCE:

Employees, vendors, and trade contractors are expected to dress in an appropriate, professional manner in order to present a positive image to all with whom they come in contact. Some things to remember include

- If applicable, representatives should always wear a clean and neat uniform that includes either a name tag or other identification feature on the front. No other pins or decorations should be worn. During hot weather, keep a spare uniform in the service vehicle in the event a change of clothing is necessary.
- Other grooming standards include clean hair, nails, well-groomed facial hair, and appropriate use of colognes and/or deodorant. Extreme jewelry, hair styles or coloring, and clothing styles are considered inappropriate.
- It may be necessary to wear sunglasses when meeting with customers. The sunglasses should be removed when speaking to customers so that good eye contact can be established.

BREAKS AND MEALS:

- Confine eating and drinking to a designated area where you are not visible to customers. Gum-chewing and smoking are never allowed in front of customers and are allowed only in designated areas.

CUSTOMER COMMUNICATIONS:

Communication is the foundation of all relationships. Verbal and nonverbal messages convey meaning to the customer. Paying attention to the tone of voice and body language, along with the actual words used, can enhance customer relationships.

- Avoid such distracting mannerisms as leaning on objects or structures, propping feet on desks or other furniture items, or keeping hands in pockets.
- Establish rapport and genuine concern by maintaining eye contact at all times and projecting a friendly and respectful attitude. Smile and use other positive facial expressions.
- Use a warm, friendly tone of voice, with a suitable volume, that demonstrates sincere interest in the customer.
- Using obscenities or arguing in a loud, overbearing voice within hearing distance of employees or customers is not permitted.
- Vendor and builder representatives will meet once per week to discuss project status and ensure a clear, open communication channel for resolving any conflicts or problems.
- Vendors providing after-move-in warranty service at a customer's home will provide the builder's service representative, within 30 minutes of work completion, a verbal status report of work done, followed by a written report within 48 hours.
- Any vendor who will be late in arriving at the customer's home to perform after-move-in warranty service must notify the customer or the builder's customer service representative as soon as possible, but no later than 15 minutes prior to the scheduled arrival time.

COMPANY PROPERTY:

- Vendors who are provided with company property, such as tools or other equipment, are responsible for maintaining the equipment in good working condition.

OTHER:

- _____
- _____

We agree to maintain the standards outlined above and understand that any violation may result in termination of our services.

Dated: _____   By: _____

Figure 5-7 Analyzing Critical Contact Points

Service Dimensions	Customer Expectations (Satisfaction)	Detracts From (Dissatisfaction)	Adds to (Exceeds Expectations)
Accessibility	The customer calls one central number; immediate response; real person answers and does not transfer the call.	The customer has to call more than once to get through; the customer cannot get out of the automated voice attendant to speak with real person.	Customer information is immediately pulled up on a database; CSR is able to confirm that everything is correct.
Communication	CSR answers the telephone in a voice that is clear and pleasant; CSR uses a friendly tone.	CSR mumbles and is difficult to understand; CSR uses builder acronyms unfamiliar to the customer.	CSR explains exactly what will happen next and when it will take place.
Competence	CSR seems helpful and willing to listen to the problem; CSR knows the warranty program and service process.	CSR has to ask questions of someone else before service request can be completed.	CSR indicates familiarity with the community and the providers responsible for requests.
Courtesy	CSR is polite and respectful of the customer's time.	CSR schedules the service at a time convenient for the provider, but not the customer.	CSR schedules at a time convenient for the customer.
Credibility	CSR understands the nature of the emergency and the process for expediting such requests.	Customer feels like the CSR is in a hurry to dismiss the customer.	CSR advises what to do until the service provider arrives.
Reliability	Service request is honored and the problem is fixed the first time.	Service provider fails to arrive at the designated time; call-back required because job not completed right the first time.	Service provider follows up to ensure everything is operating properly.
Responsiveness	CSR provides reasonable date for service on first call.	CSR is unable to give a specific time and date for service performance.	CSR communicates a sense of urgency; provider arrives ahead of schedule.
Security	CSR does not disclose occupant's work hours or times away from home.	CSR requires customer to leave a key so service provider can enter home.	CSR asks if there are any pets or other constraints to be aware of.
Tangibles	Service provider leaves documentation of work performed.	Service provider fails to leave any documentation regarding work performed.	Service provider leaves a legible and accurate copy of all work performed.
Understanding the Customer	CSR uses customer's name and pronounces it correctly.	CSR mispronounces customer's name.	CSR inquires about other family members.

Summary

Defined standards are important for effective customer service because they provide direction for how service providers should deal with customers, and they establish a measure of overall performance in achieving the organization's goals. With adequate research and understanding of a builder's customers, appropriate written standards can be established that define the performance required from employees and other service providers to satisfy those customers and achieve the objectives of the organization. Establishing standards and monitoring performance measured against those standards are essential to achieving the service quality levels required for good customer service.

S E R V I C E   A S S E S S M E N T

1. What are service standards, and how do you set them?
2. Assess the type of standards that are already in place for the different business lines or departments in your organization.
3. What are the dimensions of quality service?

Communicating About Service

We purchased our first new home several years ago. Like all new home buyers, we felt totally unprepared when it came to making the "options decisions," commitments that we would have to live with for a very long time. Some things, such as cabinetry finish and stair railings, were easy. Others, such as computer-network wiring ("How do I know where my computer and printer will go? Do I really need a network connection in the garage?"), were more difficult. After we had spent an entire weekend looking at blueprints, and mentally arranging our existing furniture along with our anticipated future purchases, we finally came to some decisions and made the commitment with our sales representative.

After we'd spent so much time in discussion and deliberation, imagine our surprise when we found the security-alarm panel installed on the wrong wall of our bedroom! As we stared in disbelief at the panel's new location, we decided the mistake was not that devastating after all. Logic took over, and we rationalized the contractor's decision to overrule our request. In fact, the more we looked at the location, the more we liked it. With a sense of relief, we told our sales representative there was no need to change the location back to our original request.

As our closing date got closer, we anxiously monitored the construction progress, including the installation progress of all the design options we had chosen early on. Everything seemed to be coming together without a hitch, until we walked into the bedroom. Staring at us as we walked through the entry into the room was the security panel, moved back to the originally requested, but now undesirable, location. How could that have happened? After all our rationalization about the mistaken placement, this new location was now totally unacceptable. Obviously, somewhere along the way, was a failure to communicate!

It was once said "a leader can't ignore his communications any more than a driver can forget to maintain the oil in his engine. The car will run briefly without outward signs of damage, until suddenly overheated parts burn out the engine. Neglect them, and damaging consequences will quickly appear."[1] The car may appear to run okay under normal conditions, but the engine may break down the first time greater demands are placed on it or more extreme operating conditions are encountered. So it is with communications inside any organization. When communications are weak, the organization may plod along seemingly okay under normal conditions, but something is likely to fail as soon as the workload increases, or at the first sign of a crisis. Without the organizational lubricant that effective communications provide, the best intentions can break down under stress and quickly damage the company's business operations and its relations with customers. This analogy is as true today as when Chester Burger first suggested it in 1964, in his book *Survival in the Executive Jungle.*

Importance of Quality Communication

Good communication with employees, customers, and vendors is fundamental to the successful operation of any organization. Keeping customers properly informed about the organization itself and about the status of goods and services that the customer may be using now or in the future is essential. If employees are to be expected to achieve a common goal, it should be self-evident that, as a group of people working in cooperation, they must have a clear and common understanding of where they are headed and how they are going to get there. In a typical organization that involves large numbers of people, the challenge of achieving the required level of understanding with all participants at several different locations is magnified many times over. Good communication becomes critical to maintaining the cooperation and teamwork needed to accomplish the organization's goals, build good customer relations, and operate at a competitive and profitable level of efficiency.

Effective communication achieves a number of key objectives that are critical to almost any organization's success. Effective communication:

- Conveys information
- Establishes an image and identity
- Motivates staff
- Maintains focus on goals and standards
- Facilitates monitoring and feedback on results
- Provides the necessary social and emotional interaction to build and maintain effective teamwork

Every organization has the need to provide large amounts of information daily to customers and employees alike. For customers, this communication might take the form of routine information available on demand, such as company background, product-information sheets, and pricing, together with more specific information such as order status or completion schedules. Information employees need includes anything that might be necessary to support the customer and the product, as well as detail about the day-to-day operation of the company and the employees' roles in it. Often, the formal brochures, presentations, and product information that marketing groups prepare are the primary means for conveying to customers the image the organization hopes to portray to the outside world.

Communication plays an essential role in staff motivation. Continuous message and information exchange about the organization's goals, business practices, and methods for dealing with customers helps to raise awareness of these subjects with employees. All too often, businesses take for granted that employees know and understand the company mission and goals. But team members who are continually kept aware of their organization's goals and the role they are expected to play in implementing those goals tend to feel personally empowered and become much more motivated to help achieve the organizational goals. These employees better understand the organization's business objectives and why they are important to the company's success. Continuous communication provides the opportunity to reinforce organization values and policies. Interaction with customers provides feedback on how well these objectives are being achieved. Employees need to hear how committed management is to customers, and they regularly need to hear the feedback that customers provide to management.

Leaders who continually interact with employees to become aware of their problems and how they need help will be rewarded with employees who are eager to help prospective buyers in the same way. By the same token, if leaders regularly communicate what is happening in their organizations, they will, in turn, find that employees are better able to help the buying public because they, too, are more aware of important changes within the organization or the business environment that could affect their customers. Continuous communication by management conveys a level of professionalism and consideration for employees that translates into the same type of positive attitude and respect for customers by those employees. Customers, in turn, feel they are valued by all who come in contact with them. Finally, when leaders support and stand behind the decisions of their employees, those front-line ambassadors show buyers that they can count on the company and all its representatives to deliver on their promises.

Work-group communication provides an important social and personal interaction essential for good teambuilding. Free and open communication between work-group members allows them to share information from common experiences, aids in problem solving, and establishes personal bonds that help co-workers work together better for customers' benefit. The bottom line is that effective communication with employees, trade contractors, vendors, and customers is a key strategy for business growth because of its effect on building loyalty, attracting new customers, and gaining referrals or repeat business.

Even though communication is one of the most important elements in the process of teambuilding and relationship development, it is also the key activity most frequently neglected in many customer-service initiatives. To create a good communication environment as part of an overall business strategy, we must understand the fundamental elements of the communication process.

Communication Defined

Communication is such a natural part of our daily lives that discussing it might seem too fundamental. Yet, when it comes to employee and customer conflicts, communication is usually the root cause of the problems. So, as basic as they are, communications concepts require some dedicated time and energy, especially from a leadership perspective.

As Figure 6-1 shows, *Funk and Wagnall's Standard College Dictionary* defines communication as "the transmission or exchange of ideas . . . or messages between places or persons."[2] In its most basic form, this process involves a sender, the message, a transmission medium, and a receiver, among which the message is conveyed.

Some communication methods do take this form, wherein the purpose is simply to convey basic information from one source to another, without consideration for how well the information might be received and understood. In most cases, however, the communication process is substantially more complex. To achieve basic objectives, communication can be all one way, as is the case with marketing brochures or newsletters. However, the most effective communication is two way, with dialogue between two or more people, which allows for feedback from the recipient to ensure that the message is properly received and understood. Figure 6-2 shows a diagram of this type of communication process. In this situation, communication involves a sender, the message, the transmission medium, a receiver, and an interactive feedback path between the sender and receiver. The additional element that disrupts communication is interference, which comes from a number of factors that can distort or get in the way of successful transfer and understanding of the message.

Barriers to Communication

Regardless of the method chosen, it is true that communication often fails to convey the intended message and meaning to the recipient. There are a number

Figure 6-1 Communication Defined

com-mū-ni-cā-tion   *n.* 1. The transmission or exchange of ideas, information, etc. as by speech or writing. 2. A means of transmitting messages between places or persons.

--Standard College Dictionary

Figure 6-2 Communication Process

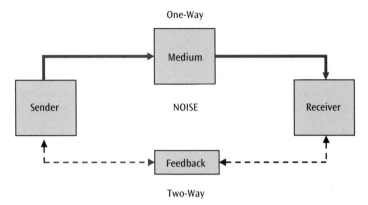

of sources for communication interference, all of which can get in the way of the intended message:

- Differences in perception between sender and receiver
- Appropriateness of the method chosen for the audience and message
- Credibility and consistency of the source with the message
- Relevance of the message to the audience
- Withholding of critical information
- Individual personality and communication styles
- Language incompatibility
- Physical structure of the work environment

In one-way communication, the sender has little opportunity to clarify or correct any misperceptions. The message received is the recipient's interpretation. This is frequently the situation when messages are sent to employees who, in turn, interpret the communications with their own filters. In the absence of any feedback mechanism for clarification, the rumor mill and office grapevines start operating, quickly and furiously.

Two-way communication, although much better, is still not immune to extensive interference that can disrupt message reception. The goal to keep in mind is that all communications must effectively produce a definite or desired result. This means that the thoughts or ideas transmitted from a sender to a receiver must be:

- Transmitted accurately
- Presented with the meaning the sender intended
- Interpreted with the same meaning by the receiver

Nowhere is this message more important than in the business world, where the original company vision is transmitted to customers through the filters of the company's employees.

How We Communicate

Today's technology-enhanced organizations use a variety of communication methods. Two broad classes of organizational communication, internal and external, are defined by their primary audiences. *External communication* is more commonly associated with promotional activity, required financial disclosures, and creation of the image that the organization presents to the general public, including customers at large, the press, and various regulatory agencies.

External communications are normally the domain of an organization's marketing department, and they usually follow specific procedures carefully screened for trademark compliance, consistency with established standards, and conformance to securities regulations that restrict the content and method by which certain information can be communicated to the investing public.

Internal communication refers to all the information transfer that might take place within the organization, between employees, management, vendors, and customers in the transaction of normal business activities. Many of the characteristics of communication are common to both types, but internal communication is considered to have the most influence on employees, and it ultimately can have the greatest impact on an organization's effectiveness.

Formal and Informal Communication

Internal communication may take several forms. *Formal communication,* for the most part, is defined by stated policies or established procedures and is often used to convey information about company activities, projects, and policies. This is often the first form of communication new employees receive. Managers who are too busy to fully acclimate new hires will often provide them, on their first day on the job, with copies of every company marketing brochure, industry article, and policy and procedure manual ever written, with instructions to read the materials to learn about the company's inner workings. Left on their own, however, new employees have ample time to develop their own interpretations of the company's culture, based only on what they read.

Informal communication is the more common and widespread form of less-structured information transfer that results from the organization's day-to-day activities. Informal communication can consist of a quick hallway conversation, numerous telephone calls and regular e-mails, or side discussions about personal or work issues that occur as part of other meetings. The infamous rumor mill is one less desirable by-product of informal communication. Appropriate use of both formal and informal communication methods will ensure that the company culture, service standards, and expectations are effectively communicated.

Communication Hierarchy

Communication moves both horizontally and vertically, as shown in Figure 6-3. When communication occurs between peers who share common goals and perform similar jobs across a work group, it is said to be *horizontal.* This type of communication flow is usually beneficial and encouraged as a way to improve knowledge and efficiency at the individual and group level, but it is also the least-controlled type of organizational communication.

Figure 6-3 Communication Paths

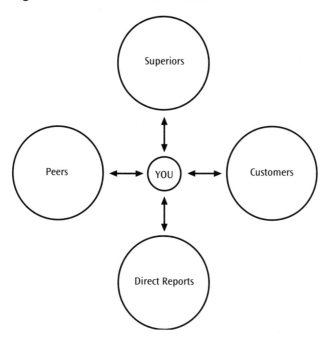

Communication can also flow *vertically* downward from management to staff or upward from staff to management, following some type of hierarchical procedure that defines how communication happens between these different levels. Organizations in which the CEO has a true "open door" policy attempt to turn the vertical process into a more horizontal and open communication channel. Because there are natural barriers to communication between people with different levels of authority and responsibility within the organization, the success of this approach varies, depending on the culture of the company and the relationship that management maintains with employees.

In an ideal business world, the working relationships are solid enough that communication flows freely in both directions, horizontally and vertically, especially when it comes to customer-service issues. All too often, though, communication is downward, with management mandating certain practices, and with no corresponding flow of information back to management about the results of those practices.

A study was conducted with the help of Sidney Yoshida, a quality expert in Japan, which has profound implications for the importance of multidirectional communications.[3] The study concluded that, in terms of knowing what problems exist within an organization, top managers were aware of only 4 percent of such problems, an almost insignificant number. Figure 6-4 shows which groups in the organization possess the greatest knowledge about problem areas.[4] Whether that mother lode of information is shared depends on the choices today's business leaders make. As builders would say, these are the options: Managers can

Figure 6-4 Problem Awareness Scale

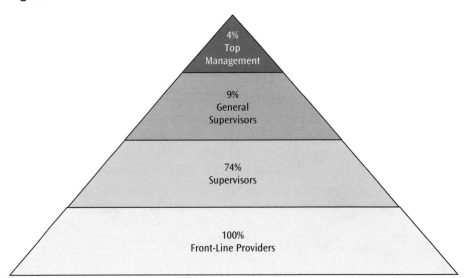

keep their doors closed with their heads buried; they can engage in one-way communication that lulls them into a false sense of achievement as communication leaders; or they can foster a culture that emphasizes and rewards open communication without punishing the message or the messenger.

Implicit and Explicit Information

In direct communication between groups of people, the actual words spoken convey a literal, or explicit, message, and such things as body language, gestures, or tone of voice also communicate indirect, or implicit, information. A typical face-to-face discussion will include transfer of both verbal and non-verbal information. A high percentage of information is contained in the non-literal cues, so nonverbal communication becomes an important part of the communication process that is lost in less personal forms of communication. Figure 6-5 shows that, when people receive a mixed communication message, they place the most emphasis on body language, followed by tone of voice, and they place the least amount of emphasis on the words themselves.[5] Other research found the results even more astonishing, with 65 percent of the message coming from body language.[6]

Communication Approaches

From the discussion above, one might presume that certain communication techniques are more successful than others, depending on the situation. This is a correct assumption. Fortunately, a variety of communication methods are available to organizations in today's sophisticated media and business environ-

**Figure 6-5 The Impact of
Communication Elements**

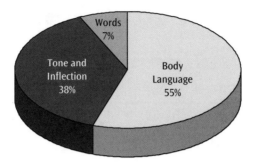

ment. Previously established methods have been complemented by continual advances in technology. These changes have dramatically expanded the available options for communicating with others. The following is a partial list of available methods we can use to facilitate communication within our organizations and with customers:

- Information brochures
- Newsletters
- Fax memos
- Voice-mail messages
- Videotape, CD, or DVD presentations
- E-mail memos
- Training programs
- Telephone calls or group conferences
- Videoconferences
- Internet-based meetings
- Direct face-to-face meetings

The Communication Richness Scale in Figure 6-6 shows the relative value and effectiveness of the different types of communication methods widely used.[7] Beginning at the low end of the scale are the more generic vehicles, such as flyers, bulletins, and newsletters. These methods work well to convey general information to a broad audience when little is known ahead of time about the audience makeup and characteristics. These media include information about items such as product updates, news events or success stories, and special promotions. These items might be disseminated by mail to a wide audience or displayed in public places such as cafeterias or libraries for potential readers to pick up if they are interested.

Glossy brochures and newsletters have high marketing appeal—and they are still widely used—although their purpose is often more with external audiences for establishing the perception of an organization's image than for specific information transfer to those inside an organization. Direct-mail letters and tailored reports can be slightly more personal forms of communication

Figure 6-6 Communication Richness Scale

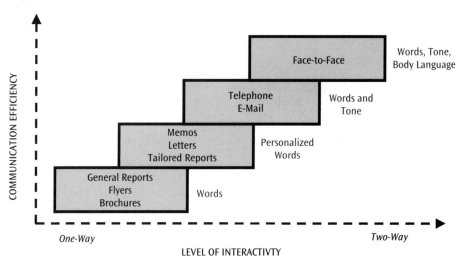

because names, demographics, affinity groups, and other personal information about the individual can be associated with them. These methods are slightly more effective and content rich than the flyers, bulletins, and newsletters noted above. However, in this era of high automation, they are sometimes so over-used, especially direct-mail approaches, that the attractiveness of the personal-ization is lost.

All of the above-mentioned communication vehicles have several common deficiencies. They are not tailored to the specific needs of each individual, and so the messages they include may not be well-matched to the perspective of the receiver and may be interpreted much differently than the sender intended. In addition, the information transfer that occurs is one-dimensional, moving only from sender to receiver, which precludes any opportunity for message clarifica-tion between sender and receiver.

The one-directional "push" methods previously described are increasingly being replaced by communication methods that more precisely target specific audiences. This targeting allows for more effective messages and, more impor-tantly, interaction with the audience, to further tailor the message and provide immediate feedback. DVDs, CDs, the Internet, and internal company (Intranet) information sites all provide methods for communicating highly customized information and messages to employees and customers alike.

That people are more responsive to, and better retain, information when they are personally involved in the communication, and when the subject is made rel-evant to their situation, is well known. When any form of communication can be made bidirectional and interactive, it becomes much more effective and allows for immediate personalization, clarification, and feedback. Figure 6-7 shows graphically how the use of a multisensory approach results in increased message retention.[8]

Figure 6-7 Message Retention Rates

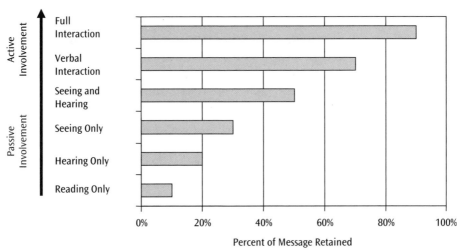

Percent of Message Retained

Fifty years ago, the telephone was the most common method of two-way communication. However, with the advent of technology, electronic mail, or e-mail, has become the new darling of the communications age and is quickly surpassing the telephone for popularity in business use. E-mail allows for a greater number of messages to be sent more quickly, at lower cost, and with a higher degree of personalization than was possible with previous methods. Yet this medium, like any other, can become overused and turn into a negative that ends up offending employees and customers—all in the interest of efficiency.

Because of e-mail's rapid adoption, most companies have allowed its usage to propagate without establishing any standards for that use. Not everyone understands the new e-mail language that includes unfamiliar characters and symbols. Well-established grammar and punctuation rules are set aside in favor of a casualness that includes elimination of capital letters and the addition of smiley-face icons. But because words are the only communication element on the screen, e-mail users must choose their words with even greater care than usual. And e-mails often are passed along or forwarded to others without the original sender's knowledge.

E-mail has become a widely used professional communications medium, and it should be treated as such. Establishing parameters for e-mail usage can help enhance communication efforts within an organization. Users should be made aware that e-mails are rarely secure and are usually backed up automatically on networked systems, so thoughtless messages that senders believe to be confidential can become incriminating documents that other parties can still access, even after senders and recipients have deleted them from their computers. Senders also should avoid long lists of people in their distribution of messages unless the email is actually intended as a group announcement. Otherwise, they should send e-mails only to those who have direct involvement in the content. In other words, don't copy everyone in the organization on the messages you send, and don't use e-mail messages to avoid face-to-face discussions of uncomfortable, confidential, or even confrontational, issues.

Internal e-mail communication is affected by the outside world, as well. Those unsolicited bulk e-mails—known in the electronic community as *spam*—that mysteriously appear in electronic mailboxes are taking their toll on American business. For example, recent reports from CNET News attribute 36 percent of all incoming e-mail to spam.[9]

Sorting through the mounds of unwanted messages is a daily ritual for employees, who often inadvertently delete important messages in their quest to rid their computers of additional visual clutter. This process takes time away from other activities and also puts a drain on the company's bandwidth and storage infrastructure. Software applications are available to help reduce spam, although eliminating it entirely is difficult.

Other technology-driven, labor-saving devices are intended to improve communication, but they can actually have the opposite effect when they are used inappropriately. Computerized telephone-call systems with pre-recorded messages are a good case in point. Prospecting for customers this way allows no opportunity for relationship building and, in fact, often antagonizes the customer. Nothing is more frustrating than answering a telephone that greets you with a prerecorded, canned message from someone who is pretending to be interested in you and your well being.

One day, I decided to test the effectiveness of this medium by listening to the entire message from a random call I had received. The voice on the other end was touting the interest rates he could offer for a home loan whose payments would be far lower than my current payment. (How did he know my current interest rate? He wouldn't even talk to me in person!) The voice instructed me to stay on the line if I wanted further information, and a representative would join to help me. Admittedly, because I was more curious about the computerized system than the interest rates, I stayed on the line as instructed, eager to see what would happen. The tape recording ended, and, after a few moments, a telephone started ringing on the other end. My curiosity quickly abated after the twelfth ring and ended when I terminated the connection. Not only did the caller miss an opportunity for true interactive communication, but the company image was tarnished in the process.

Telephone solicitations have become such an overused nuisance that more than 42 million people have pre-registered with the government's recently established National Do Not Call List in an attempt to minimize this type of communication coming into their homes.[10]

Technology overused can lead to customers abused.

The bottom line for service providers to remember is that technology overused can lead to customers abused.

Use of computer automation can provide unique opportunities for better customer interactions, even when only machines are involved. My bank has a method for making the ATM experience seem a little friendlier and more personal. Each menu selection in the ATM transaction requires time for the system to process. During this brief delay, a friendly message pops up to say, "Thank you, I'm working on that." The airline that lost my luggage used an even more innovative technique, which is a variation on the one the bank uses. Through a completely automated process, the airline asked callers a seemingly endless stream of questions. To have their answers recorded, callers were instructed to use the numeric keypad for their responses. Callers were rewarded with the sound of simulated keyboard strokes on a computer as they entered the numbers; this provided audible feedback and crudely simulated the response of a real, live, customer-service representative. At least this approach indicates an awareness that something needs to be done to personalize these one-dimensional forms of communication. A research study conducted by Purdue University found that using interactive voice-response units instead of touchtone interactions shortened banking calls by 35 percent and reduced costs significantly. When *speech recognition* (in which customers speak directly into the handset rather than use a numeric keypad to respond) was used, the unit cost was 45 cents, compared to almost $4.00 when an agent handled the call.[11]

The richest and most versatile form of communication is person-to-person, face-to-face interaction. Although this may be the most time-consuming and costly method, much of the information that results from actually meeting with customers and employees cannot be easily obtained using any of the other methods available. The ability to interact with another individual or groups of people, getting to know them personally, seeing their responses in both humorous and serious situations, reading their body language, and hearing their tone of voices, is invaluable. The audio-visual cues and personal interaction fills in the data, opinion gaps, and raw statistics that are lacking with other communication techniques.

Proactive leaders spend a lot of time meeting with staff and visiting customers often and early in the sales cycle. Effective managers may regularly man customer-service request lines, or even periodically cover other sales functions that involve customer interaction, all in the interest of communicating. The message sent to employees and customers with this kind of management involvement is highly positive, and this approach can return benefits equal to or greater than many well-orchestrated public-relations campaigns.

Effective Communications for the Home Builder

When it comes to communication about customer service, the home builder's organization is faced with many of the same communication problems that any other organization encounters. The home builder faces additional communication hurdles and even greater reliance on effective communication, however, because of the mix of direct employees, outside representatives, and independent contractors over which the home builder exercises only limited control. This complex of people makes good communication essential to coordinate these disparate groups and build a team that shares the same values, objectives, and schedule priorities necessary to provide good customer service.

In customer-satisfaction surveys, the top-ranked builders consistently receive highest ratings for the quality of their communications with customers, suppliers, and employees.[12] These surveys also suggest that employees tend to mirror the behaviors and actions of their organizational leadership, especially when the credibility of the message is firmly established by management backing up the messages with clear actions. When communicating management's commitment to customer service, there is no substitute for leading by example. The communication precedents management establishes with employees, determines to a great extent, how the employees will treat the builder's customers. Further, there seems to be a high correlation between employee loyalty and customer loyalty, with effective communication the key to developing this loyalty from both groups.

The home builder cannot overlook the importance of good communications with the service partners who have direct contact with the customer before, during, or after the home purchase. These people are all closely woven in a web that represents the builder, with effective communication the key to maintaining the builder's standards, getting feedback, and keeping customers satisfied. For example, in its surveys of 18,000 post-occupancy buyers, Eliant research found that the areas in which customers were least satisfied involved poor communication by the sales and lender personnel during escrow.[13] This was especially true of first-time buyers, but even 27 percent of those who previously had been through the process experienced dissatisfaction with the quality of communication from these providers.

The most recent industry study conducted by Eliant in partnership with *Big Builder* magazine reinforces the impact salesperson communication has on builder referral rates. Two issues out of 11 are communication-related and contribute more than 50 percent to a buyer's consideration of whether to refer other buyers:[14]

1. Buyers want to know that the salesperson is looking out for the buyers' interests as well as the builder's. This impression is conveyed through demonstrated consistency between words and actions. When promises are made, those promises must be kept. Discerning buyers will detect even the slightest body-language or intonation nuance, and this discrepancy will have an impact on the buyers' impression, either positively or negatively.

2. Another critical characteristic is whether the salesperson proactively keeps buyers informed of construction progress. Buying a new home is an emotionally draining experience for most people. Add that to the stresses of everyday living, and you have people who are often totally irrational. When salespeople regularly communicate construction progress, they remove uncertainties and ease tensions that often are escalated in the absence of information.

Summary

Effective communication is one of the most essential elements for successful organizations to master. Top management must have a good understanding of the communication process, available methods, and barriers to communication if it is to champion and promote good communication techniques to others within the organization. Good communication is essential for the home builder because that is how the builder coordinates activities and maintains standards for the actions of all the contractors, agents, and representatives who are involved in supporting the customer on behalf of the builder. Good customer service is all about making sure that the expectations customers carry through the door have not only been met, but are exceeded, by the time they complete the purchase cycle. Effective communication is the key, both to providing good customer service and to exceeding those service expectations.

SERVICE ASSESSMENT

1. Assess your current level of communication effectiveness by having all managers administer the following survey in their departments. When the surveys are completed, compile and disseminate the results to determine areas of weakness. What steps will you take to improve the areas of weakness?

SURVEY DIRECTIONS:

Read each statement carefully and consider how much you agree or disagree. Using the following scale, circle the number in the column that best describes your perception of your department. After completing the survey, please take a few minutes to answer the three questions that follow.

continued on next page

1 = Strongly Disagree		2 = Mildly Disagree		
3 = Mildly Agree		4 = Strongly Agree		

Communicating about Service

1. Our senior- and middle-management teams have frequent contact with past and existing customers.   1 2 3 4
2. We have frequent all-company meetings in which everyone gets together for regular updates on customers and the status of the organization.   1 2 3 4
3. Employees can describe the company vision and guiding values.   1 2 3 4
4. Employee expectations are clearly communicated.   1 2 3 4
5. The management team's words and actions are consistent when it comes to delivering exceptional service.   1 2 3 4
6. Employees know exactly what customers expect from their service experience with the company.   1 2 3 4
7. Employees are free to cross the departmental boundaries and chain-of-command when it comes to providing service to external customers.   1 2 3 4

Total point value of all numbers circled in this section

Percentage (Total ÷ 28)   %

A. In what ways have you seen communication breakdowns cause service failures in this organization/department?
B. How do you think communication among employees and departments could be improved?
C. How could communication to external customers be improved?

2. Identify any external service partners who communicate directly with your customers before, during, or after the home purchase. In addition to reviewing their practices to ensure consistency with your communication standards, do the following:
   A. Determine how often those service providers proactively communicate with your customers.
   B. Verify the customer-satisfaction levels for these service partners with either internal or external research.
   C. Collaborate with these service partners to devise an action plan for correcting any communication-service deficiencies.

Delivering Quality Service

**THIS CHAPTER COVERS THE
FOLLOWING CONCEPTS:**

1. Factors important to
   delivering quality
   service.

2. Enabling providers.

3. Continuous monitoring
   of service delivery.

4. Considerations for the
   builder.

Introduction

In these days of economic turmoil, everyone is looking for some way to maximize the return on their investments. I am no different, which is why an online brokerage firm seemed attractive to me. The company's advertisements, website, and promotional materials all proclaimed how much the company valued its customers. This sounded like a great company to deal with. With the image of service extraordinaire so effectively established in my mind, I moved quickly to open an IRA account, so it could be finalized before the tax-year deadline. The online application proved to be easy to complete and submit, just as promised. My follow-up telephone contact confirmed that the application had indeed been received. However, before the account could be opened, the company had to receive my completed IRS form. The service representative gave me instructions for how to download the form and concluded the conversation with a sincere "Thank you very much; we appreciate your business." This was impressive, and, so far, seemed to confirm that this was a company that actually lived up to the image its marketing group had created.

After I had faxed the completed paperwork, I made another follow-up telephone call to verify that the company had received the necessary forms. At this point, the first crack in the customer-service armor appeared. The customer-service representative informed me that the company had, in fact, not received my faxed paperwork. "Are you sure?" was my question. In my mind, I pictured stacks of unretrieved faxes sitting in a box—or, worse yet, an empty paper tray waiting for replenishment. The account representative apparently didn't appreciate me telling her that I was holding a transmission report that confirmed the time my fax was sent and received. Her only response was, "We didn't receive it." This time there was no "We appreciate your business" at the end of the conversation, only "It will take 24 to 48 hours to process your request, depending on how many other applications we receive." Gosh, if they are that busy, maybe my business really isn't all that important.

Because I was working under a deadline to get the account opened, I placed another call to confirm that the company had received the second set of paperwork I sent. This time, the response was much different. Yes, it had been received, everything was in order, and the account would be opened in 24 hours. The conversation even concluded with the now-familiar "Thank you very much; we appreciate your business." What a relief! At least the company "almost" lived up to its word. One minor service failure wasn't too bad, considering how service goes most of the time.

Now somewhat cautious because of my earlier experience, I placed another call 24 hours later, just to make sure everything was in order. Imagine my surprise when the customer-service representative told me that the account could not be opened because I had sent the wrong IRS form. How could that be? I followed the instructions of the first customer-service representative precisely. Unfortunately, "the computer" was showing that the account could not be opened until the new form was sent. The representative repeated to me the same downloading instructions of two days ago, directing me to the same section on the company website. When I questioned whether the account could be opened today if the information was sent immediately, I heard the same familiar refrain of "It will take 24 to 48 hours to process your request, depending on how many other applications we receive." And finally, "Is there anything else we can do for you?" A tiny voice inside me wanted to shout, "No, you idiot! I can't even get an account opened! Why would I want to complicate my life even further?" Knowing that would do no good and, most likely, would make matters worse, I politely declined his offer. This time, the same "Thank you for calling, and we appreciate your business" closing didn't sound quite as sincere as it had the first time.

Factors Important to Quality Service

If an organization has followed all of the steps of the Service Synergy Model to this point, the next stage, the delivery of service, is where the rubber meets the road. Developing a vision, identifying service partners, understanding the true needs of customers, creating service standards, and, finally, effective communication are all critical service elements, but they aren't enough to turn a mediocre company into one with a strong service delivery. Individuals must be motivated and equipped to handle their awesome responsibilities. In my experience, it was obvious that the brokerage representatives had received some type of customer-service training, because they were able to parrot the company mantra of appreciation for customers and the business they generate. Yet, when it came to opening accounts—one of the company's key services—they failed badly in the delivery.

Although the people on the front line are charged with the actual execution of service, the company leader has a key role in assuring that the service delivery meets the standards outlined. James Belasco and Ralph Stayer, authors of *Flight of the Buffalo,* were correct in their assessment when they said, "The people own the responsibility for delivering great performance, and I own the responsibility for creating the environment where this ownership takes place."[1] Most leaders know that monitoring income statements and balance sheets are part of their everyday life, but without delivery of the company's core products or services, the balance-sheet numbers will start moving in a direction that gives shareholders and other stakeholders cause for concern. One of the best ways to keep the numbers going in the right direction, and a strategy that is within the company leader's control, is to create a work environment in which employees are motivated to perform. They will do so when they know what is expected of them, when they are empowered to solve problems, and when they are prepared to recover from service failures if they occur.

The old adage, "A picture is worth a thousand words," speaks volumes about how leaders can get their people to take ownership of service delivery. No matter how clearly a service standard is written, or how often senior managers talk about the importance of exceptional service delivery, there is nothing like living role models to demonstrate what good service looks like. Words on a paper are subject to interpretation, especially if they are not clear and concise. Cultivating service mentors to exemplify service delivery puts action behind words and paints a living picture. Role models are the people who symbolize the organization's service standards; they are mentors for others to follow. Their day-to-day actions bring the service culture to life and personify the organization's strength. They are the achievers who demonstrate the kind of behavior that is expected, whether they are delivering service internally or externally.

Enabling Providers

The best service can falter without employees who are not fully dedicated to delivering the best service possible. Employee attitude differentiates one group from another. Even under the best of circumstances, service delivery may be sabotaged if managers fail to address the motivation of the employees, contractors, and vendors who are part of the service-delivery process.

Yet how to motivate staff is a dilemma, a question that is pondered every day. "How do I motivate my employees?" surfaces regularly, but rarely does an answer provide concrete actions for managers to take. There's a good reason for that. Managers are asking the wrong question. The correct question is "How do I get my employees to motivate themselves?"

Motivation is not something managers can do for their employees. As much as they would like to control this aspect of service delivery, the act of motivating employees is beyond their control. All employees are motivated to do something, but it is usually what they want to do and not necessarily what managers want them to do. Peter Block summed it up in his book *The Empowered Manager* when he said, "The source of all energy, passion, motivation, and an internally generated desire to do good work is our own feeling about what we are doing."[2] In other words, we cannot motivate employees; they motivate themselves. More about self-motivation will be discussed in Chapter 8, but the one motivator within a manager's control is the ability to create an environment that encourages employees to carry out the service standards that are consistent with the company's culture. When the environment is right, employees are eager to assume responsibility for their own performance and accept personal accountability for delivering exceptional service.

Clarifying Expectations

One of the best ways to motivate people is to make very clear what is expected of them. Work expectations are those activities and outcomes that represent the desired production output for an employee's specific job. Whether spoken or unspoken, these expectations become the key drivers of attitudes, which in turn influence job performance, commitment, and satisfaction.

All employees hope to gain something from a working business relationship, either now or in the future. It may be career growth, opportunities for new experiences, or just the pleasure they derive from doing something they enjoy. Whatever the rationale, they come to their new job situations with mental pictures of what will happen throughout the course of that relationship. Obviously, when new employees join an organization, they—along with their new managers—have expectations of how their jobs will be performed. Both have already visualized what will happen in the work situation. Unfortunately, the two pictures may be very different, because people draw their expectations from their own perspectives. The sources of those perspectives can include previous jobs, movies they have seen, books they have read, or even classes they have attended. It is up to managers to bridge any gaps between what both parties believe "should" happen and what actually does. New employees are not much different from customers buying our products. If there is a gap between what the customers expect and what they actually receive, there is dissatisfaction, and the customers will go away. Likewise, if new employees become frustrated with the work environment because it hasn't lived up to the promised expectations, they will exit, too.

Written service standards, which are the second step of the Service Synergy Model, are the solution for managing any conflicting expectations. If these standards are clearly written with strong performance outcomes, any subsequent problems with service delivery will be minimized. In their *Work Expectations Profile Research Report,* Inscape Publishing identifies three separate studies that have shown that employees who have well-defined and clearly communicated job expectations find more satisfaction and success in their work than those employees whose job expectations are loosely defined or ambiguous. Organizations that employ satisfied, successful people are likely to enjoy increased productivity and reduced turnover in their work forces.[3]

An organization is only as strong as its weakest link. That means there must be consistency in service delivery among everyone who is part of the operation. Two managers who have similar responsibilities in different offices cannot maintain their own sets of standards. There's nothing wrong with enhancing and improving upon the core standards, but the core standards serve as the minimal level of performance, and they must be consistent from location to location. The lack of standardization creates confusion for employees who may transfer to a different office. Customers who see inconsistency from one community to another will also question whether this same inconsistency occurs in the construction quality of the builder's homes. Once a standard is compromised without any response from management or the customer, that level of performance may become the new standard. Alternatively, careful communication coupled with solid mentoring will quickly turn a new employee into one who is a contributing ambassador of the company's service philosophy.

Empowering Your People

Even high-performing service ambassadors will occasionally come up against unusual customer problems. These situations, which are outside the boundaries of normal standards, require quick action on the part of the service provider. This point was made very clear to me while I was standing in the express line of the grocery store one day. The gentleman in front of me watched carefully as the clerk scanned his items for checkout. When the price of his pint of raspberries scanned at $3.99, he was quick to point out that the display sign in the produce section showed the price to be $.99. Running the container past the scanning device once again, the clerk told the customer that $3.99 was actually the correct price. Learning of the new price, the gentleman told her to exclude the item from his order because he no longer wanted the raspberries at that price. This critical contact became a key decision milestone. The clerk could either have ignored the customer's obvious embarrassment over the situation, and allowed him to leave without the raspberries, or she could have charged him the lower price. Charging the lower price wasn't in the best interests of the store, because other customers might try to take unfair advantage of the store by repeating a similar scenario.

The clerk's split-second decision at this point proved to be an outstanding example of empowerment. She first told the customer that computers sometimes make mistakes, and so she wanted to go over and check the produce section herself. This simple act demonstrated she was looking out for the company's best interests, but she also acknowledged to the customer that he might be correct. After a few moments, she returned to the station with a wide smile on her face. "The correct price is $3.99, but the sign for the strawberries, which are $.99, got moved in front of the raspberries. That was clearly our mistake, so please take the raspberries at $.99." You could tell by the smile on the customer's face that the decision was well received. He was satisfied, and there was no doubt the store retained the loyalty of that customer.

On-the-spot problem solving by empowered employees is a key factor in delivering the kind of service that will keep employees happy. Policy manuals try to define appropriate actions for "normal" customer problems, but not every situation can be anticipated. And often, the situations that benefit most from empowered employees aren't even that unusual. They are simply new situations that the service provider has never encountered. Hearing service providers say "I'll have to check with my manager" is a signal that the employee has no power to make a decision, and there will be a delay in resolution for the customer. The time between problem discovery and problem resolution is often long enough for the customer to become dissatisfied enough to find someone else who can deliver the same, or perhaps even better, service. The response from my brokerage company was a prime example. When I learned of the company's apparent indifference in expediting my account, it was only a matter of minutes until I found another firm down the street that promised to complete the entire transaction in 30 minutes. The brokerage company lost an opportunity to gain a new customer because of its inability to offer an expedited solution to my problem. No one wanted to take ownership of the problem because employees were not empowered to make a decision. Every day, companies throughout the country lose similar opportunities to maintain satisfied, loyal customers and any referrals that might come with them.

Customers want to know that the person they are dealing with has the ability, creativity, and license to go outside of the policies and procedures manual when it is in the best interests of the customer and the company. Employees' ability to quickly respond to exceptions or unusual customer requests is critical. TARP's research conducted in the late 1990s found that 82 percent of customers with problems will buy again if the complaint is resolved quickly, compared with only 54 percent whose complaints are simply resolved.[4]

Clearly, the key is to empower employees with the authority to make decisions that are in the best interests of the customer. That can be an unnerving thought, especially for the manager who has difficulty giving up control. Empowerment is a two-way process that takes place in the stages shown in Figure 7-1. Managers who want to develop service-oriented mindsets in their employees must first determine whether they are ready to empower

Permission and protection go together. others. Before they can give away the power to make customer-centered decisions, managers must first give their employees permission to do so, and then they must be prepared to give employees protection in the event they make a mistake in the process. Permission and protection go together. The first time an employee receives a stern reprimand for making a decision that "isn't the way I would do it" is the last time that employee will ever risk making a mistake by going beyond the normal procedures in an attempt to satisfy the customer.

Figure 7-1 Stages of Empowerment

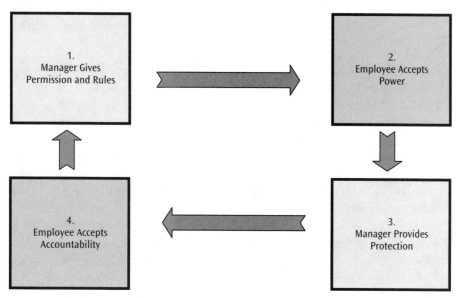

Managers need to set aside their egos and evaluate the end result of employees' actions. Too often, the focus is on the path taken to achieve the results rather than the result itself. Everyone knows more than one road leads to most destinations. Using employee initiative to better satisfy customers in a way that is consistent with company goals should be encouraged, not punished. Remember, the important thing is the result. Did we provide good customer service that turned an unhappy customer into one who is satisfied, loyal, and enthusiastic enough to continue to purchase additional products and refer others to our establishment?

Empowerment is a powerful tool for motivation. When managers bestow this type of authority on their employees, they are sending a powerful message that says, "I respect you, and I trust your judgment to know when to take initiative and be creative in your day-to-day dealings." Just as landscaping needs to be thoughtfully planned and nurtured, so do empowered employees. Empowerment isn't successful unless a supportive and encouraging environment exists.

Some employees relish the idea of empowerment because it gives them a license to solve problems immediately. However, employees have to remember that every license comes with inherent responsibilities. Those who accept empowerment must stand ready to be held accountable for their actions. Empowerment doesn't mean there's an open checkbook for making customer problems go away. Sound decisions can be made only in an atmosphere in which employees know the rules of empowerment:

1. They must understand the company's vision and the role each department plays in turning that vision into a reality.
2. Goals must be clear and concise, leaving nothing to question.

3. The values that guide and dictate employee actions need to be articulated and demonstrated daily.
4. Limits of authority and procedures for handling unusual service requests must be identified.

When those four conditions are in place, employees will be ready to accept empowerment and the accountability that goes along with it.

The fundamental requirement for successful empowerment is trust. If employees cannot be trusted, managers will attempt to control every outcome. Conversely, if employees feel their management team cannot be trusted to back up their decisions, employee willingness to take risks and be proactive will remain low, hampering productivity and impeding their ability to support any but routine customer situations. Trust is mutual, and it is the one characteristic that takes a long time to build, is easily destroyed, and is even more difficult to regain.

The diagram in Figure 7-2 shows the five elements that build trust in an organization, with integrity and competence serving as the cornerstones. These intangible characteristics are sometimes difficult to describe. *Integrity* is the degree of honesty and truthfulness consistently displayed by someone; integrity is the most important characteristic for determining trustworthiness. *Competence,* another critical dimension for trust, refers to the technical and interpersonal skills required to do a job. Once leaders display their technical ability to do a job, others will enthusiastically follow. When their technical skills are combined with the interpersonal skills that demonstrate how to get things done through others, leaders possesses a powerful attribute that will set the stage for fostering trust. *Consistency, loyalty,* and *openness* make up the remaining dimensions of trust.[5]

Looking at each dimension in greater detail, we know that consistency is demonstrated when employees see their managers as reliable, predictable, and using good judgment in handling situations. Employees watch their managers very carefully because they are the primary role models. Unpredictable emotional outbursts violate this dimension and will result in employees taking little risk because of the potentially unpredictable response from management. Without that risk, managers are doomed to solve every problem themselves, which will result in unacceptable delays in the resolution of customer problems.

Any employee dealing with a multitude of customers will periodically make mistakes. Loyalty is reinforced when managers protect their employees and even allow them to save face during times of adversity. Remaining loyal to the employee who never makes a mistake is easy. Maintaining loyalty to those who struggle

Figure 7-2 Elements of Trust

through valuable learning experiences on their way to empowerment is more difficult.

Finally, sharing information freely and willingly creates an environment of openness that produces further bonds of trust. Employees have greater confidence when they know they have the right information from which to make sound decisions. Information is a valuable resource that helps people do their jobs better. One of the greatest management faults is not providing employees with adequate information about the company and the business. For example, it is always surprising when departmental leaders are held accountable for meeting certain profitability targets, but then management holds back from them, as confidential, some of the overhead-cost information that directly affects their bottom line. This double standard leads to fragmentation and territorial thinking, as employees see only their department and not the rest of the picture. Whether they are part of an internal support group or one that has direct contact with the customer, all employees need to see how their jobs and their departments fit into the big picture. When all five elements are present and working in concert, trust is built. And if one element is broken, it will take an even longer time to repair the damage than if trust had not been established to begin with.

Identifying Policies That Are Barriers to Service Delivery

Well-designed customer-service plans and motivated employees are essential to delivering good customer service, but even the best of strategies won't succeed if an excessive number of obstacles stand in the way of providing service to the customer. Unintentional barriers block motivation. Motivational barriers can range from serious infrastructure issues to simple behavioral annoyances. No matter what the cause, the end result is still the same: a demotivated employee operating at suboptimal productivity.

Based on our own research with employee focus groups, most barriers can be categorized into the four areas shown in Figure 7-3:

- Insufficient communication by management
- Inadequate internal systems, processes, and infrastructure
- Inefficient resource allocation and utilization
- Deficient individual skills

A valuable technique for identifying service barriers is to conduct a simple audit to understand what inadvertent or institutional obstacles may be standing in the way of effective service delivery. A surprising number of perceived barriers are actually simple annoyances that become major issues when time is at a premium and employees are dealing with many priorities. Often, once they are identified, these minor annoyances can be eliminated with very little cost or effort. Other barriers, such as internal information-processing systems, hiring processes, and organizational structure, are more complex and may require more detailed analysis, formation of a task force, or additional investment in equipment to correct.

Figure 7-3 Service Barriers

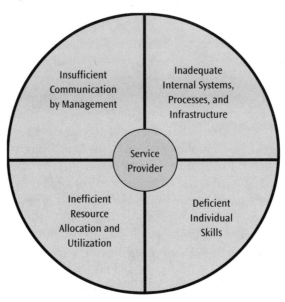

As an example, one perceived barrier is the complaint heard all too frequently that managers do not say hello to their employees in the morning. The first time I heard this complaint, it seemed humorous, but the same refrain has been echoed so often that it seems to have become a standard business practice. One employee told me very clearly, "When my boss comes in, he walks right past me and never even says good morning. Why should I go out of my way to show courtesy to customers, when he won't go out of his way to do the same for his employees?" This is not the best way to foster a positive attitude in your front-line service providers, although this type of oversight happens all too frequently.

One hospital group was frustrated because its patient-tracking systems were inconsistent and outdated. The hospital had achieved significant growth through acquisition over the past 10 years. When it came time to standardize the technology infrastructure so that everyone was using the same systems, there was so much resistance from the different user groups that nothing was changed. The end result was that three independent systems had to be accessed before a patient could check in for services because none of the systems was able to share data with the others.

Another service group was consistently at odds with a different department that appeared to continually monopolize the company copy machine with its large projects. Both groups felt the solution was for each to have its own expensive copy machine. Although the first group viewed this dilemma as a significant barrier to good service, the problem was easily solved with a simple "courtesy" policy. Now, anyone who has a large project is required to inform colleagues in advance, through a group e-mail list, how long the copy machine will be inaccessible. With advance notification, everyone can plan copy schedules accordingly. This was a simple barrier to remove once it became apparent that it was a service issue. Unfortunately, the problem came to light only when the manager proactively asked about it.

Given the current state of business, with the necessity for strict cost containment, one red flag should be raised and waved in front of every manager as a major wake-up call. A surprising number of people who attend my customer-service classes feel their capabilities are underused and could be applied more productively. In some cases, these employees have voiced their frustrations to management. In other cases, they have not. Those who have stepped forward find their frustrations increasing if nothing is done to give them greater responsibility or job enrichment. Being proactive has become a punishment, because their ideas are being ignored. Those who don't bother to come forward with their concerns of underuse are simply biding their time, giving what they perceive as a day's work in exchange for a paycheck until something better comes along.

Regardless of how well a company is managed, it seems there are always employees who are overly sensitive to the various barriers, and who allow those barriers to affect their productivity and performance. Too many times, employees are saddled with a "bad attitude" moniker, when in fact their frustration with unresolved barriers is affecting their attitude and the quality of service delivery. A negative attitude is a symptom of a greater problem. When no one takes the time to ask about service barriers, companies run the risk of leaving unnecessary barriers in place, and they miss out on key opportunities to create a more stimulating work environment with highly productive and motivated employees.

Conducting a service-barrier audit is one of the easiest ways to correct problems. Posing the question "What's getting in your way of delivering good service?" at an office staff meeting is well worth the time investment. Asking this question will yield concrete input, make employees feel that their ideas are valued, and, most importantly, improve service delivery. Remember, however, that a caveat is attached to the question. If you ask it, you must be prepared to act on the responses you are given, or else you will lose credibility with employees.

Creating a Service Recovery Plan

No matter how clearly empowered employees are, it is reasonable to expect that not all customers will be satisfied with the responses they are given, especially if a problem situation becomes escalated. The "lost" brokerage firm experienced just that. The second service representative set the stage for my future expectations. She cast doubt on the credibility of the firm from the time we spoke. The outcome would have been far different if she had just said, "For some reason, we haven't received your paperwork, but I can do one of two things for you. It will take me about an hour, but I can put a tracer on this to see what happened, or you could resend the fax right now to a different number, which is a direct line to our new-accounts department. Which would you prefer?" By not giving me these kinds of options, and placing the blame squarely on my shoulders for the paperwork not getting into the appropriate hands, she escalated the situation and planted the seed of doubt that my original provider choice was not a good one.

Perhaps my reaction was irrational, but given the size of my deposit, which would surely contribute to the firm's profits and help pay the representative's salary, my expectations were a little higher. The point is that the few seconds or hours after a mistake is made can be the single most-important opportunity for creating loyal customers. When something goes wrong—and it certainly will—the follow-up after the incident, not the fact that the problem occurred, will leave the most lasting impression on the customer.

No one should deliberately expect to fail in the delivery of service. Obviously, service failures are undesirable, but they can have a positive side if they are handled properly. Rather than panicking at the first sign of customer dissatisfaction, providers should view the situation as an opportunity for recovery. Those customers whose complaints are resolved with good customer service can actually become significantly more loyal than those who had no problem at all.[6] This situation is the time to show customers the truth about those marketing phrases and jingles that attracted the customers in the first place. Service recovery will be successful only when employees are equipped with the tact and diplomacy skills for handling those situations in which customers may be unpleasant, highly distressed, and emotional.

Maintaining a complaint database provides a wealth of information for anticipating the causes of dissatisfaction. Without accurate records, identifying whether the system or individuals are at fault becomes impossible. And whatever the cause, the recovery plan must be quick, proactive, and consistent from one service provider to another.

Continuous Monitoring of Service Delivery

Golfers know exactly how far they need to hit a ball each time they step up to a tee, because the yardage information is provided on scorecards and markers. Armed with that knowledge, they can select the right club to get the job done. Service providers also need some kind of indicator that will show them what the target is, so they can determine how to reach it. Performance measurements are powerful tools for motivating others to reach the highest levels of achievement and remain accountable for their actions. The caution is to make the measurements meaningful, consistent with corporate goals, and simple to track, because what you measure is what you will get.

For example, many call-center representatives are evaluated on the number of calls they take. Obviously, this number is simple to track, but, standing alone, it may actually work to a company's detriment. If service providers are so focused on the number of calls they handle, they may sacrifice other traits such as courtesy, consideration, and listening in the process. This very practice is evident when telemarketers hang up mid-sentence after it becomes obvious to them that their services are not desired. Yet they can make the argument that they met the performance measure. A more effective measure would combine number of calls handled with customer-feedback surveys.

The natural tendency is for leaders to establish the measures and then impart them to their groups. Although this method saves time, it also reduces the level of buy-in and commitment from those who are responsible for achieving these performance levels. A more effective method is to work with the service providers to help them develop their own relevant measurement systems. Once these systems in place, the providers can begin charting their own progress and making continuous improvements until they achieve the target.

Establishing service measurements is not an easy exercise, especially if customer needs are not well understood. The process can be time-consuming, which is precisely why so few companies do it properly. But people want to be engaged in their organizations so they can contribute and make a difference. No one intentionally delivers poor service; but without appropriate benchmarks, the risk of that happening is high.

Considerations for the Builder

Today's builders have a lengthy, complex service cycle that involves employees, trade contractors, vendors, and numerous partners who play a key role in the process. What is most important to remember is that service delivery does not end when home buyers move into their homes. In fact, research by Eliant found that builders who scored highest in satisfaction were unusually sensitive to their customers' needs at four separate points in the service cycle—the design phase, during the sales process, during the escrow period, and after move-in:[7]

1. The best builders think of their customers long before the product is designed, by conducting focus groups to understand the characteristics and features that are most important to them. Builders want to be able to anticipate challenges so they in turn can prepare their customer-contact people. It's all about understanding what customers want, the first step of the Service Synergy Model.
2. The importance of communication and the role of the salesperson during the sales process cannot be overemphasized. Buyers are screaming for proactive communication, quick responses to phone calls, and honest information that demonstrates someone is looking out for their best interests.
3. The period of time between purchase and closing is one of the most trying for buyers. It is filled with legal and regulatory jargon that seems like a foreign language. No buyers want to appear as though they don't understand every piece of paper they sign, especially given the large investment they are making. Sensitive salespeople and lenders know they will have lower cancellation or fallout rates if they take the time to explain—in a language that is easily understood—all the processes and procedures that will happen during the loan-processing period.

4. Everyone always feels a sense of satisfaction and elation when the keys are finally turned over to a new homeowner. The tendency is to think of the "closing" as the end of the transaction. Builders who possess that mind-set, however, will probably not receive the highest scores on customer-satisfaction surveys. Eliant uncovered the true importance of this phase on a buyer's willingness to refer others to the builder. After move-in, a buyer's most pressing concerns for up to one year are with the quality of repairs, clean up during and after repairs, and the timeframe for completing these repairs. More than 41 percent of a customer's decision to refer is based on the results of these factors.[8] In the past, builders have focused most of their service-delivery attention on the sales process and the period up to 90 days after the sale. Armed with this new information, the implication for builders is that the service-delivery cycle should extend through the first year of ownership.

Summary

After focusing on the definition of effective customer-service systems, policies, and strategy for the organization, managers can start to address the actual implementation of these policies through the service-delivery process. To create the most conducive environment for delivering good customer service, an organization needs to define clear expectations for employees, and then provide those employees with the autonomous authority to quickly resolve unforeseen issues that may arise during interactions with customers. It is also important to identify and remove any incidental or systemic barriers that interfere with the service delivery. Because service failures cannot be totally eliminated, it is essential to plan for and emphasize the value of service recovery when initial problems occur. Continuous monitoring of the quality of service provided, using a variety of measures, will help to refine the process and ensure that good customer service is consistently delivered.

SERVICE ASSESSMENT

1. What factors are important to delivering quality service?
2. Identify unusual situations that employees could encounter in the course of delivering service. What should be said to the customer, and how should those situations be handled?
3. How can your company continue to monitor service delivery?

Maintaining the Service Culture

Introduction

After we moved to a new home several years ago, it became apparent that our family needed a new bank. A community bank located nearby attracted me with its innovative radio commercials that touted the difference between this bank and "the other guys." Those 60-second spots had me "laughing all the way to the bank." On my first visit, I found that the promise of personal attention from people who enjoy their jobs and have fun working with customers carried through to the bank representatives who greeted me at the doors. What a surprise! The bank's words were backed up by the actions of its employees. The relationship was satisfying until several years later, when my little bank was acquired by a larger regional bank. Even though a new name appeared on the door, many of the faces did not change, and so I expected the level of service I had experienced in the past to continue, even with the new management.

Over time, however, subtle changes started taking place. New policies started coming from the corporate office with some regularity. The smiling faces that used to greet me were slowly replaced with less-friendly faces whose owners sometimes complained about headquarters changing the old policies and adding new fees. Only procrastination and some residual loyalty to my old bank kept me from moving my accounts. Then, I heard that my little community bank had been acquired again, this time by an international player in the world of banking. The change this time was even more dramatic and rapid than the first.

Now, when I walk into the bank, instead of scowling faces, I'm greeted with a telephone and a sign that says, "Pick up the phone, and you will be connected with a representative." There are still in-person service representatives, but they never make eye contact or acknowledge customers. In fact, one teller slammed her window in my face just as I was approaching because it was time for her to take a break. This occurred even though there were no other customers in the branch. And my request would have taken her less than 60 seconds.

From the community bank to the international conglomerate, there has been a gradual erosion of the culture and qualities that built the bank and made it attractive to me in the first place. The original service-oriented culture that once appealed to me is now nonexistent, having been replaced by something entirely different. Whether intentional or not, the culture has changed from one of "customer" appreciation to one of "account" appreciation. To show my appreciation for the change in the customer-service culture, I am moving my accounts to another bank that seems more customer-oriented and seems to have values more consistent with those of my original bank.

Maintaining the Corporate Culture

Maintaining a service culture is much like trying to maintain the original codes, covenants, and restrictions that go along with a new-home community. A lot of effort goes into designing the original layout and look of the development. Those people who are the first owners and who share in the excitement of seeing vacant land turn into a community of well-landscaped, pristine homes are only too willing to see the standards maintained. After all, this is what they bought. The expectation is that certain rules and regulations will be followed to maintain the integrity of the developer's vision, whether the purchase is new or resale.

After awhile, many of the original owners move out, and new owners take their places. Although the new owners like the look and feel of the community they just purchased into, they probably haven't been informed and don't bother to learn about the existing standards for their community, and so they don't really have much knowledge about what went into creating the original community style. Their attachment to the original design standards is much lower because they were not part of the community evolution. Sometimes, their desired modifications are contrary to the existing architectural standards and regulations already in place. They may even believe the regulations are silly and do not really pertain to them. They also know that if they ask the association architectural committee for permission to modify any regulations, their requests will be rejected. Consequently, a mentality of "It is better to ask forgiveness than permission" prevails. No matter what the motivation, the first time a restriction is violated, the standards of the community start to erode. If such violations are left unchecked, the codes and restrictions will become meaningless, with the violations establishing the new benchmarks for what is acceptable in the community.

A company's service-oriented culture is much like the new-home community and the codes, covenants, and restrictions that go with it. The organization's culture, with its standards and guiding values, is in place; but the people, like the neighborhood, change with time. New people eventually replace those who must leave, creating a new dynamic when they are combined with those who stay. The new members must now become acclimated to the existing standards and practices, while the existing members need periodic attention to keep them invigorated. Without that, the original vision will wither and eventually fade away due to neglect.

Methods for Sustaining the Culture

Maintaining an organizational culture that embraces customer-centered strategies is only possible if the employees who are charged with executing these strategies understand and adopt the same underlying cultural values that company founders visualized. After all, they are now the ones responsible for successfully managing the critical contacts and developing long-lasting customer relationships. Hiring, training, and retaining good employees is a three-point formula for ensuring continuation of an established customer-service culture. All efforts to define, document, and establish a strong customer-oriented service culture will be wasted if the culture is not adequately maintained during employee turnover and the constant change the organization will surely face.

In the beginning, the organization's leadership becomes the primary driver for establishing and championing the culture, but a strong management team is what provides the crucial link in supporting and maintaining the culture as it evolves. Management must have strong buy-in to the culture and be willing to work continuously to communicate the basis for and importance of supporting the cultural values to others in the organization. In their book *Corporate Cultures,* authors Terrence Deal and Allan Kennedy found three factors that differentiated the culture-centered manager from those managers who place little or no emphasis on the culture:[1]

1. Culture-centered managers are sensitive to the long-term impact the corporate culture can have on the organization's success. They are constantly talking about the culture, both inside and outside the organization. Whether the culture is mentioned in an annual report, staff meetings, or marketing materials, these managers credit cultural strength for market success. Less-successful managers might see this as inappropriate "cheerleading" behavior. Thinking the culture is unimportant and that promoting it is secondary to their duties, they may be embarrassed to openly promote the corporate culture with other team members within and outside the organization when, in fact, it is one of the most fundamental and important activities they should be engaged in.

2. Culture-centered managers use the cultural values as a binding factor for building trust, teamwork, and synergy. These are exactly the reasons for having the well-defined culture in the first place. When everyone is held to the same standard of performance and accountability, trust between team members is more likely to develop, and people work together better in recognition of a common goal. No obstacle is too difficult to overcome because it is "us against them" rather than "me alone." Trusted employees take greater individual ownership and responsibility for maintaining the culture and values of the organization.

3. Culture-centered managers see themselves as the flag-wavers and standard-bearers in the daily parade of service opportunities. They recognize the importance of culture and see the number of times during the day when they have an opportunity to demonstrate their commitment to the service culture.

These managers know that, to deliver good customer service consistently and at every opportunity, they must obtain, train, and retain the right people.

Good Service Starts with Good People

The initial hiring decision is the starting point for ensuring that the right people will be available in the organization to support and sustain its culture. Some people possess the nature and temperament to be good service providers. They genuinely like people and view service problems as a challenge they can overcome to the mutual benefit of everyone concerned. They are comfortable being proactive, and they work well within a generally defined set of parameters. Conversely, some people work better in a more structured environment, with minimal customer contact. They prefer to avoid confrontational situations that involve uncertainty and conflict. When managers are making hiring decisions, there are many factors to consider besides the actual technical skills required for the job. These factors include personality traits, work preference, and, most importantly, that the candidate's cultural style and values fit with those of the organization. Employee turnover is a reality in every organization, but finding a replacement for an open position goes beyond looking only at technical skills and experience. Instead, managers should focus on hiring for values and work ethic first because "more workers are fired for poor attitudes and lack of discipline than for lack of ability."[2]

Some time ago, The Carnegie Foundation completed a study to identify those personal attributes that contribute to a person's success in a particular occupation. The surprising results, shown in Figure 8-1, indicate that success factors on the job are only about 15 percent due to a person's actual job or technical knowledge, whereas 85 percent of these factors can be attributed to interpersonal and self-management skills.[3] Technical knowledge alone is not nearly enough if someone does not possess the interpersonal skills to deal with peers and customers who could benefit from that knowledge. Further, if the person cannot be trusted to use his or her own initiative when applying the knowledge in inter-

Figure 8-1 Required Skill Set for Success

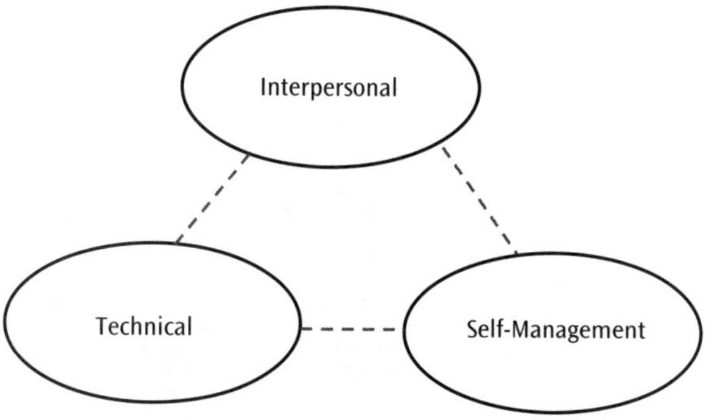

action with other people, but instead has to be closely managed at every turn, the value the individual brings to the organization is dramatically reduced.

The Hiring Process

When reviewing potential job candidates, even if a manager is fortunate to receive a multitude of resumes to select from, finding the right person can still seem like looking for a needle in a haystack. The sheer volume and, often, lack of differentiation between candidates can make recruiting new employees a time-consuming and discouraging process. This leads many managers to give up in frustration and make their selection based on superficial qualities, or, worse yet, their gut instinct. It is important to put a sound hiring process in place to give fair consideration to all suitable applicants, and to greatly increase the odds of finding the right match in a reasonable timeframe.

Just as your customers go through a decision track that contains critical contact points along the way, the hiring process can be represented in similar fashion as a series of sequential actions and decision points, as shown in Figure 8-2. Analyzing your hiring process in this way will help identify problem areas that prevent you from finding the right candidate relatively quickly.

Creation of a standardized hiring process provides a number of advantages for the organization that can help sustain the culture as new employees are added. Following consistent procedures ensures that candidates are given fair and equal consideration, so that good candidates are not inadvertently overlooked because of otherwise minor negatives. Formal procedures ensure that all candidates are treated with appropriate courtesy and respect, regardless of their qualifications. Even though candidates who apply for a specific position may not be a good fit for that position, they still may be prime candidates for other positions in the future, or they may be able to refer contacts who would be qualified candidates for the current position. Job candidates learn about your organization from the interview process, and so they could end up providing referrals or actually becoming customers for your organization's products in the future, based on the opinion they form during the recruiting activity. Following a standardized

Figure 8-2 Hiring-Process Decision Track

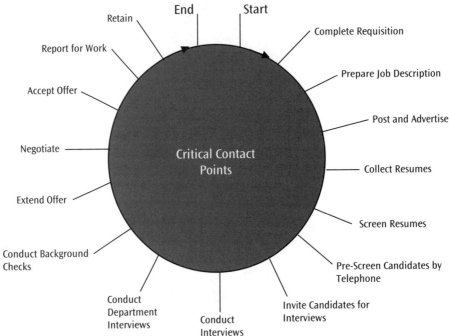

hiring process also ensures that the best candidate is obtained while the company conforms to legally required procedures. At the same time, the company is represented in the best possible way to preserve a relationship with someone who could become a future employee or customer.

Developing Job Descriptions

A properly written job description is the first step to take in standardizing the hiring process. When written effectively, the job description can assist in establishing salary parameters, determining interviewing criteria, communicating duties and responsibilities, writing concise recruitment advertising, and even supporting the company with documentation in the event of unlawful termination or discrimination lawsuits.

The job description should detail the critical skills and background needed for an individual to perform the job well to the standards established by the company. The job description should also not overlook a description of required values and cultural characteristics, and it should emphasize the need for a good fit with those of the employee. There's no doubt that technical skills are important, but today's service providers don't work in a vacuum. They must interact with customers, coworkers, vendors, and suppliers to solve problems and get quality products in the hands of buyers, elevating the importance of interpersonal skills such as communication, time management, negotiation, and customer relations. These are all important job requirements, and they should not be ignored.

The manager should conduct an honest assessment to determine the types of work habits and traits that will create a successful partnership between employer and employee. Is it the ability to withstand pressure or be adaptable to frequent change? Do employees need to act in an entrepreneurial manner, acting independently, but treating the company's business as though it were their own? Realigning the emphasis on interpersonal skills and cultural fit, as shown in Figure 8-3, will save time and money in the long run because costly hiring mistakes can be avoided by ensuring a good cultural fit with each new hire.

Processing Resumes

In the shrinking job market prevalent over the past few years, getting applicants to respond to an open job position has not been a difficult task. One manager who ran a Sunday ad in a large regional newspaper found 200 resumes waiting in his electronic mailbox when he arrived for work the following morning. The Internet makes it easy to post and apply for jobs. The danger with this reality is that quality drops as quantity goes up. Many people broadcast their resumes broadly, even for those job openings for which they are obviously not qualified, in the hope that something will click. Traditional resources such as newspaper advertising still work, but the return on the investment can be less than satisfactory. One of the most reliable resource pools for finding potential candidates is from your current employee base. The likelihood that successful employees know others like themselves is high, making a referral-incentive program for current employees a useful and cost-effective tool to aid in recruiting good talent.

The next step in the hiring process is to review resumes and determine whether candidates match targeted job requirements. This in itself is not a difficult task, but the hiring manager should have a screening process in place so the results can be as purely objective as possible.

Figure 8-3 Skill Set Pyramid

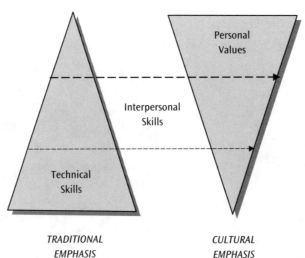

TRADITIONAL
EMPHASIS

CULTURAL
EMPHASIS

Time is valuable, and you probably will not be able to read every resume that crosses your desk. You should be able to screen an applicant's resume quickly for key elements. If the background appears to be a close fit for the job requirements, the resume merits review based on the other criteria listed in Figure 8-4. Establishing a consistent pattern for reading resumes will help you establish an objective method for determining which candidates you will ultimately interview.

Develop a "process of elimination" for reading resumes. Start with Yes and No piles. On the first pass, look first for the required skills. If the resume includes the technical skills you need, place it in the Yes pile. If the resume does not include the technical skills of the job description, it goes in the No pile. Sometimes, candidates will mention their interpersonal skills, but this is more likely something to determine during the face-to-face interview.

To help you deal with the volume of resumes typical in today's environment, and to provide consistency and objectivity in the initial prescreening process, many companies are now using software that can automatically process scanned or electronically formatted resumes. This software screens for key words that represent traits necessary for the job at hand. Automation using appropriate software tools can eliminate the need for at least some of the initial screening described above, which allows the manager to focus more quickly on the most likely candidates.

Conducting Interviews

Another area that requires consistency to ensure that candidates are selected objectively based on the same job criteria is the interview process. That all candidates be asked the same questions is critical. Preparing interview questions in advance—and then asking the same ones of each candidate—becomes one of the keys to consistent, effective interviews. One mistake that hiring managers make is to let the candidate lead the questioning away from the planned direc-

Figure 8-4 Resume Checklist

What to Look For	Red Flags
☑ Previous Employers	↝ Employment Gaps
☑ Education	↝ Job Hopping
☑ Employment History	↝ Fluctuating Income
☑ Thoroughness	↝ Reason for Leaving a Previous Job
☑ Neatness	↝ Incomplete Application
☑ Organization	↝ Industry-Changing Pattern
☑ Stability	
☑ Technical Skills	
☑ Income Pattern	

Establishing a consistent pattern for reading resumes will help you establish an objective method for determining which candidates are ultimately interviewed.

tion. Although this sometimes can yield useful information about that candidate, if the discussion deviates too far from the planned line of questioning, critical questions may not be asked and the result can be a difficult "apples to oranges" situation when comparing one candidate to another.

Once the interviewer has gathered basic information about a candidate's education, work experience, previous positions, job changes, and levels of responsibility, he or she is ready to evaluate the candidate for interpersonal skills and cultural fit. In addition to the traditional interviewing questions, another technique called *behavioral interviewing*[4] will be useful to gain greater insights and help to further determine the cultural fit of a candidate. This popular method of interviewing was developed by industrial psychologist Dr. Paul Green and is used by companies throughout the country. Behavioral interviewing complements more traditional approaches by exploring specific past experiences as an indicator of potential future success.

The behavioral approach to interviewing involves asking predefined questions that attempt to eliminate the canned or conjectural, and sometimes misleading, responses that candidates who are skilled speakers often provide in reply to general questions. Instead of broad questions about hypothetical situations, this type of interviewing focuses on behavioral responses, in which the candidate is asked to describe his or her past behaviors in situations similar to the problem area or issues that the interviewer is asking about. The benefit of this approach is that it asks for specific examples of previous behavior or experience; so, unless the candidate is deceptive, the response given is based on past performance that is directly applicable to the position being interviewed for and should be an indicator of potential success for that position.

Too often, hiring managers ask ambiguous or leading questions that steer the applicant and result in misleading answers, or, worse yet, answers that do little to allow for assessment of the candidate's potential for future success. "This job requires a lot of contact with customers. Do you like working with people?" is so obvious that only the most unenlightened individual would answer in the negative.

Similarly, asking potential employees about hypothetical situations yields only hypothetical responses, with no indication that candidates would actually be inclined to take, or capable of taking, the action described. For example, "What would you do if you received two emergency requests at the same time?" will yield a textbook answer sure to please anyone. The reality is this may not be applicants' actions when they are faced with the same dilemma on the job. A far better interview approach is to ask behavior-based questions that direct interviewees to give specific examples of how, in the past, they handled multiple emergency requests for service. These anecdotes allow the hiring authority to gauge the depth of understanding and range of service issues interviewees have encountered. Figure 8-5 gives examples of the difference between traditional interview questions and those that are behaviorally based.

The final step in the interview process is to provide candidates with a realistic job preview. Many managers are so eager to fill an open position that they

Figure 8-5 Traditional versus Behavioral Questions

Traditional	Behavioral
"This position requires someone with a high degree of flexibility. How are you at adapting to challenging situations?"	*"Describe a time when you had to adapt your work style to adjust to a challenging customer or situation."*
"What would you do if someone wanted to make design changes that were not allowed in the community?"	*"Tell me about a time when you had to express an idea or opinion in a very tactful way."*
"How do you go about finding solutions to problems?"	*"Give me an example when you generated several solutions to a difficult problem."*
"What would you do if an irate customer called you on the telephone complaining in a very demeaning way?"	*"What experiences have you had in dealing with irate customers? Give at least one example."*
"What would you do if you were required to work with someone you didn't really like? How would you handle it?"	*"Almost all work situations require us to interact with some people whom we dislike. Describe a situation that you have encountered like this, and explain how you handled it."*

conveniently fail to mention the "realities," focusing only on the positive aspects. For example, some jobs may require frequent overtime at certain times of the year because of the cyclical nature of the business. Telling applicants the true extent of unplanned overtime could discourage them from considering a position—and prolong the search even more—so the interviewer might skirt around the issue of extensive overtime, creating misperceptions about the job, and setting the stage for potential performance problems after the hire.

As a manager, you shouldn't be afraid to paint a realistic picture. Believe it or not, retention rates can actually improve when you do so. Your forthrightness shows the applicant that you are honest, trustworthy, and conduct yourself with integrity by painting an accurate picture of the job, both positive and negative.

Potential Roadblocks to Successful Hiring

Once you have jumped through the hoops of screening resumes and interviewing candidates, often two and three times, it is time to extend the offer. Finding exactly the right candidate after a lengthy search is highly satisfying.

But nothing will dampen that excitement more quickly than having the candidate you were so sure about reject your offer. It is too easy to blame tight labor markets or escalating salary demands for the inability to attract top candidates. The reality is that many companies are losing their best candidates because of poor communication and inconsistent procedures they have used during the hiring process. Candidates are withdrawing their candidacy from positions they first thought were highly desirable, or they are opting for competitive positions because of less-than-positive impressions they receive during the entire recruitment, interviewing, and selection process.

According to a survey sponsored by Integrity Search, Inc.,[5] top candidates drop out of the hiring race when they perceive that the hiring process is too long and complicated. The argument for having a well thought out process in place is further supported by the fact that 70 percent of the respondents to the survey felt "the interview process is a strong indicator of how a company operates." Based on the survey findings, here are four of the greatest frustrations for candidates:

1. Interviewers were not prepared and focused during interviews. Candidates frequently complain that when they are being interviewed separately by several people from the same company, they are often asked the same questions. A group interview would have resulted in the same information, would have taken less time, and would have presented a better company image.

2. Candidates found there was a lack of feedback on the status of their candidacy. Minimally, a letter or even a telephone call stating that the position is temporarily on hold, is still in consideration, or that someone else has been hired for the position is a simple courtesy that sends a powerful message. A company that takes the time to follow up with aspiring applicants is also the kind of company that would follow up with external customers, as well. Whether or not the candidate is selected, the message from such follow-up action is that the company cares about preserving a relationship with the candidate, either as a potential employee or as a customer.

3. It is hard to believe, but many candidates complained that they received no written job descriptions, or that job descriptions differed from one interview to another within the same company. In one case, a candidate was told she would write her own job description once she got on the job.

4. Finally, the last complaint candidates had was that prospective employers did not appreciate the time and energy candidates put into the process. Candidates invest many hours in the interview process, including travel time to accommodate multiple interviews, and often even use personal vacation days in the process. Something as simple as scheduling interviews after normal work hours, at the convenience of the candidates, is an act that would take most candidates by surprise and create a positive and lasting impression.

Good candidates are hard to find, no matter what the employment picture looks like, but companies cause more of their own recruiting problems than they realize. In conducting a strategy session for a company that wanted to improve its hiring process, I asked one question of each of the managers who were present. How much time elapses between position identification and the employee's first day on the job? Obviously, the time varies depending on the position, but the general consensus was that the entire process could not be completed in less than 90 days, and in most cases it took longer than that. Think about that from the candidate's perspective. How many people are willing to wait that long, given other alternatives? When people are ready for a change, they want to make it happen as quickly as possible. Quality talent is highly desirable, and the company that knows what it wants, knows where it is going, and is ready to take action will always win the talent war.

Prepare Customer-Contact People through Training

Organization leaders will tout the importance of training in their organizations, but that training is often underutilized or misapplied. According to Peter Kline and Bernard Saunders in their book *Ten Steps to a Learning Organization,* training has all too often "been an afterthought because we used it to plug up holes instead of to furnish our business with the highest quality personnel."[6] That is a powerful statement that accurately summarizes the view many organization leaders have toward training. In theory, they will argue their advocacy of training, even citing examples of programs or speakers who have been brought in from time to time; but if you look for the presence of a structured, ongoing training curriculum to back these words up, evidence is usually nowhere to be found.

In times of economic crunch, training is one of the first line items to be eliminated from a budget because of its perceived overhead cost. Training, as we will see later, does not have to be expensive. When leaders start seeing training as a process, and not a one-time event, they will start enjoying a much greater return on the costs of their training activities.

In fact, forward-thinking leaders look at training in just that way—as a process. According to a study of best practices, reported by the Federal Benchmarking Consortium,[7] the best companies view training as an ongoing investment, not an expense. They may even use their complaint-tracking systems to identify training needs for new and existing employees, to correct for deficiencies in skills and procedures that could result in great expense to the company if not addressed properly.

The age-old question of how much to spend on training is a difficult one to answer, because the investment is very dependent on the company and its unique situation, including longevity, type of product, turnover, and how rapidly the company is growing. There are many different ways to determine general guidelines for the amount of time and resources that should be committed to a training effort. As Figure 8-6 shows, three common measures are used as a benchmark. Some companies look at training expenditures as (1) a percent of payroll, (2) a specific dollar amount per employee, or (3) a predetermined number of training hours per employee. A recent study by the American Society for Training and Development found that the percent-of-payroll amount ranged from a low of 1.1 percent in the health-care category to a high of 2.6 percent in the finance, insurance, and real-estate categories. The rapidly growing, leading-edge companies that consider training as an important investment allocated as much as 3.6 percent of their payroll to training.[8]

After looking at those benchmarks, the inclination is to calculate the figure for each individual's organization. No matter which benchmark is chosen, the number needed for adequate staff training may be seen as excessive, given other priorities. However, rather than dismissing the numbers as irrelevant, a more reasoned approach is to step back, take a look at the big picture, and then start building a training curriculum in a cost-effective, results-oriented manner, considering training to be a critical long-term investment. Two factors that emphasize the importance of training to the organization cannot be overlooked:

Figure 8-6 Training Expenditures

Expenditure Ratio	Ranges for All Categories	Finance, Insurance, and Real Estate Category
Percent of Payroll	1.1% to 2.6%	2.6%
Training Dollars per Employee	$301 to $1,075	$942
Training Hours per Employee	24 to 35	29

Source: The 2000 State of the Industry Report, The American Society for Training & Development.

1. New employees must be provided with training that orients them to the organization's culture, mission, values, and performance expectations necessary to help them be successful. Too often, employers look at new-employee orientations as initial meetings with the human-resources professional to review benefits and company policies. After that, training is left up to whatever the manager chooses for the employee, along with the self-initiative of the individual worker.

2. Training for existing employees cannot be overlooked as a means to continually improve skills, increase productivity, and reinforce company values and culture. As employees grow and look for greater career opportunities with new responsibilities, training becomes a valuable benefit. Companies gain, too, because they are able to adapt to changing market conditions if they have proven employees in place who already possess the desired knowledge and motivation, but simply need updating or retraining in their technical skill sets, a task which is much easier than trying to find someone new.

For both employee groups, training is a highly desirable company benefit, often more attractive than stock options or other benefits that are part of a normal compensation package. As a motivator and key strategy for attracting new talent while retaining existing personnel, training is second to none. Companies that fail to tout their dedication to training are missing out on a key marketing opportunity for differentiating themselves in the labor marketplace and gaining a competitive advantage in the consumer marketplace.

Many companies have established themselves in this regard by forming their own corporate universities. Not to be confused with the bricks-and-mortar institutions of higher learning, a corporate university is a process, not a place. It is a method whereby all levels of employees, as well as key customers and suppliers, are involved in continuous, lifelong learning to improve their performance on the job. A properly designed corporate-university curriculum is customized to meet the specific needs of the organization, taking into consideration its mission, its customers, and its employees. This type of program will not only maintain and increase employee competence, but the very nature of its standardization also will help to promote consistent representation of the corporate culture with all employees, across different locations, offices, and business lines. Figure 8-7 outlines the basic structure of a corporate curriculum,[9]

Figure 8-7 Structure of a Corporate Curriculum

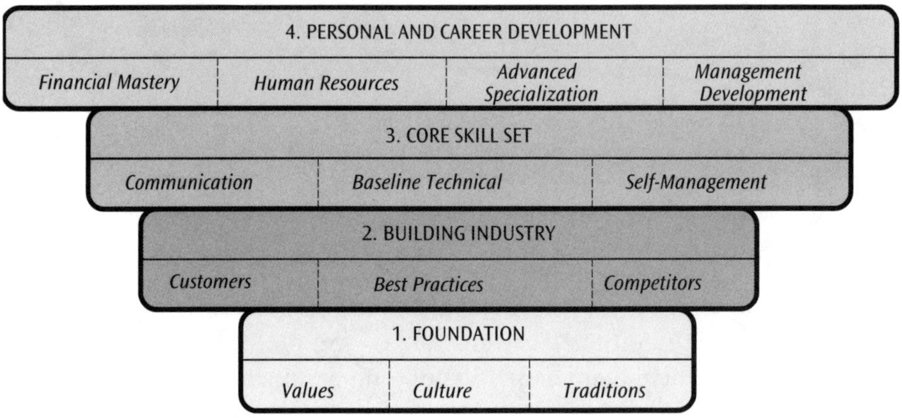

4. PERSONAL AND CAREER DEVELOPMENT			
Financial Mastery	Human Resources	Advanced Specialization	Management Development

3. CORE SKILL SET		
Communication	Baseline Technical	Self-Management

2. BUILDING INDUSTRY		
Customers	Best Practices	Competitors

1. FOUNDATION		
Values	Culture	Traditions

recognizing that each program should be adapted to the company and its primary industry.

This type of training can involve a significant start-up expense if it is viewed as requiring a traditional, full-time, internal staff. Many other approaches and methods are available as alternatives to a department of full-time staff trainers, however. Outside independent contractors who have specialized expertise in a specific area can offer a cost-effective approach when full-time services are not needed, or when training needs are immediate. Commercial providers for standard programs, Web-based distance learning, and CD-based interactive programs are other alternatives that may be suitable and more cost-effective in certain cases. Alternatively, every company has its own internal subject-matter experts, people who have operational expertise, but who also have other company-related job responsibilities. Using these internal professionals in a training capacity ensures that their valuable intellectual capital stays within the organization, and doing so allows others to gain the benefit of such positive mentoring. Those who accept the responsibility of training others are often flattered that they have been asked to share their expertise, which creates additional job enrichment and motivation for them, as well. Industry associations are another valuable source of training expertise, both for the materials developed on behalf of the membership, and for the various conferences these associations sponsor. Other popular types of training include panel discussions with top producers and clients, or even establishment of a company-wide guest speaker program made up of internal employees who share their experiences with other departments or divisions, so others in the company can benefit from these living case studies.

Technology is one other area that has allowed training to reach more people in a more cost-effective way. From video teleconferences to audio newsletters, a multitude of delivery methods exist to fit every budget, as shown in Figure 8-8.

No matter which delivery method they select, leaders must be ready to demonstrate their commitment to and support of training. Their actions will help their companies obtain a higher return on the invested training dollars. Many studies

Figure 8-8 Methods of Delivering Training

■ Staff Trainers	■ Audio Teleconferencing
■ Internal Subject-Matter Experts	■ Video Teleconferencing
■ Independent Contractors	■ Self-Paced Instruction
■ Professional Association Training	■ Job Aids
■ Panel Discussions with Top Producers	■ Audio "Newsletters"
■ Client Forums	■ Company Intranet
■ Internal Guest Speakers	■ Product Suppliers
■ Unions and Trade Associations	■ Colleges, Universities, and Community Colleges
■ Computer-Based Training Software and CDs	

have been conducted on how much training content is actually transferred to the work environment. The news is not good, with the consensus being that only 40 percent of the training program content was used in the work environment immediately after training. After six months, only about 25 percent was being applied. By the end of the year, only 15 percent was still being used.[10] Obviously, this is not a high return, and it can also explain the reluctance of some senior executives to invest large sums of money in future training endeavors.

Just as employees encounter barriers to delivering good customer service, barriers that must be removed by the company's leaders, so are there barriers to training. John Newstrom, Ph.D., investigated impediments to training and found the most significant barrier that keeps employees from transferring what they learn in the classroom to the job is lack of reinforcement. In essence, there is no incentive to use the new skills or material because no one seems to care whether or not they are used. The second most significant barrier was interference from the immediate work environment. This means that even though employees attend the training, they may be prevented from using their new skills because of other obstacles in the environment. Many training participants have returned from their sessions only to have a manager undermine the training they just attended by saying, "Now that you have gone to training, here is the way I really want you to do it." The third most significant barrier to training effectiveness identified in the study was a non-supportive culture.[11]

In any type of training, three groups of people have a vested interest in the success of the initiative: the management team, including senior management and the participant's supervisors; the participants themselves; and the people who are directly involved in delivering the training. These groups working together before, during, and after the training event create a cohesive process for guaranteeing the highest return on the training investment.

Retain Employees through Recognition

The final element that will help to perpetuate the service culture is to ensure that those highly valued employees who demonstrate consistent service excellence don't become disenchanted and move to other positions. Besides training, an important way to keep employees satisfied is through appropriate recognition of their efforts.

Positive and negative reinforcement are concepts taught in every beginning psychology class. Basically, a behavior will be repeated if you strengthen it with the addition of another stimulus, such as a reward. In theory, you will get more of whatever you reinforce, whether the behavior is positive or negative. Parents use this technique all the time in trying to get their children to act in a specific way. They give money for good grades. They award special privileges for cleaned rooms. They give recognition for good behavior. The examples are limited only by the circumstances of the child and the creativity of the parents.

Just as parents provide basic rewards for their children, employers need to provide appropriate rewards and reinforcement for desired professional behavior from their employees. It is up to the management team to understand what motivates employees, and to determine the types of rewards that will yield the most positive results. The best reinforcer for encouraging exemplary service is to recognize that service when it happens. All employees appreciate acknowledgment for a job well done. The trick is making the acknowledgment a meaningful and continuing motivator to the employee who is the recipient. Unfortunately, this is where many companies fail most often in motivating their employees.

Employees are motivated intrinsically and extrinsically. When employees are intrinsically motivated, they push themselves because the reward is an internal one that comes from engaging in the activity itself. People may be motivated by the challenge of completing a difficult task, the opportunity for freedom of expression, or by the fact that they are mastering a new skill. Extrinsic motivation comes from the promise of a specific reward for completing a task or achieving a goal. If the objective is met, employees will in turn receive tangible rewards. These rewards can include bonuses, time off, trips, free event tickets, and a host of other incentives, all designed to motivate by rewarding employees for performing at exceptional levels.

Many organizations have planned generous, extrinsic reward programs for those who demonstrate extraordinary performance. Sales managers have used this type of reward program for a long time, granting plaques and titles that recognize the employee as Salesperson of the Week/Month/Year, or something similar, to everyone who achieves the goals. Other departments have copied the practice by including their own versions of the program with an Employee of the Month or Year. These programs are nice for the person who is singled out, but what happens to the other people who were not selected? Does this mean that their performance was unacceptable? In a department of 12 people, the unspoken message is that when one person is a "winner," the other 11 people must be "losers" who have under performed. While the winner is temporarily motivated to work harder, the other 11 people will, at best, maintain status quo or even become demotivated, wondering what it will take for them to earn the plaque with their name engraved on the bronze plate. The bottom line is that extrinsic reward programs may not be the best motivators because they have a tendency to lump everyone into the same basket with the same reward, they are short-term in their results, and they are often costly to implement.

Intrinsic rewards usually take on a higher importance than actual monetary compensation, assuming that the employee is already paid fairly. Even so, intrinsic rewards are often given less consideration because they require managers and company executives to know and understand what motivates their employees individually. When companies take the time to do this, they demonstrate to employees how much they really care about them and their well being. Companies, in turn, are rewarded with employees who are more deeply committed to the organization and who accept ownership of their jobs. Feelings of satisfaction and accomplishment last much longer than the excitement of participating in a one-time event and receiving a monetary award. True motivation comes from a work environment in which people want to be engaged, accountable, and recognized for their achievements.

With or without a monetary incentive attached, employee recognition is still a powerful motivator as long as the reward is meaningful to the recipient. One manager made the mistake of rewarding everyone in his department with a dinner for two at the most expensive restaurant in town. For some, this was a special treat. However, one dedicated employee, whose husband traveled extensively, found the reward to be more of a burden. After clocking long workdays for several weeks, the most important thing to the employee was spending time at home. The employee's husband looked at the so-called reward almost as a punishment. The last thing they both wanted was to spend another night away from home. What started out as good intentions backfired. A more appropriate reward in this instance would have been a dinner catered at home for the entire family.

Service-recognition programs, whether extrinsic or intrinsic, can take numerous forms, both monetary and non-monetary. Figure 8-9 provides ideas about what other companies have used to reinforce service excellence. A poll of people in my own department brought some surprising answers that would have escaped me. The new mom with her first child wanted access to an attorney who would help her get wills drawn. Another valued team member had dreamed of a dolphin interactive experience for his wife at the local marine amusement park.

The key to recognition effectiveness is how quickly the behavior is recognized. Intrinsic rewards have greater impact because they can be given immediately instead of waiting for a specific time or company event, often long after the performance occurs. Extrinsic rewards are generally more effective when the company is trying to improve group performance and an entire team can be recognized and rewarded.

Recognition and rewards can be given for any number of actions as long as they relate to the company's goals and mission. Recognition for supporting the company's guiding values or culture is almost always appreciated if the recognition is sincere and backed up with management action. New performance records, cost reductions, service-improvement suggestions, innovation, team unity, and on-the-spot decision-making are all good recognition opportunities.

Figure 8-9 Intrinsic and Extrinsic Rewards

Characteristics	Intrinsic	Extrinsic
Description	Motivation coming from within	Motivation coming as a result of an external reward
Sample Motivators	■ Freedom from control ■ Challenge ■ Power and authority ■ Direct answers ■ Opportunities for individual accomplishments ■ Freedom from detail ■ New and varied activities	■ Event tickets ■ Meals ■ Trips ■ Gifts ■ Promotions ■ Plaques ■ Certificates ■ Parties and celebrations
Factors to Consider	■ Long-term value ■ Low cost to administer ■ Employee controls when reward is administered ■ Encourages creativity ■ Good for achieving personal goals	■ Short-term value ■ Expensive ■ Manager controls when reward is administered ■ Discourages creativity ■ Some may perceive as manipulative ■ Good for achieving group goals

Individual recognition is important, but recognizing good performers as part of a group effort also rewards the manager with a cohesive team of top performers. When handing out awards for service superiority, remember vendors and trade contractors, for they, too, are part of the service-delivery effort.

Considerations for the Builder

Today's home buyers have clearly indicated they are looking for more than just a quality home. They want to buy from home builders who have well-established, long-term, and consistent reputations both for product quality and for quality in the support they provide to their customers. To be successful, builders who have developed the types of strong customer-oriented cultures described in earlier chapters need to continually renew these cultural values because of the rapid rate of change in service-provider staff in the builder's own employ, and that of representatives the builder is associated with. As with other factors in service-culture development, the challenge for builders is to continually encourage practice of these cultural values with the various sales representatives, design-center personnel, lenders, trade contractors, and other outside personnel in the same way direct employees expect. The hiring, training, and reward techniques described previously are effective ways to maintain an established service culture for the builders' own employees.

Although home builders cannot likely exercise large influence over the hiring practices of trade contractors and representative agents, they can and should certainly include these groups in specific training efforts and motivational programs that they use with direct staff, when these techniques are also appropriate for these associated providers of customer service. Doing this will provide a double benefit, first in helping to renew and maintain the service culture, and also in building a stronger composite team, with all members focused on the same goal of providing good customer service for the builders' customers.

Summary

Establishing a highly successful customer-service culture provides little benefit to the organization if those values defined by the culture are not carried forward as the organization evolves over time. Management is key to sustaining the culture, and so recruiting a high-quality management team that is motivated and capable of promoting the organization's culture is essential. Good hiring practices that provide for careful selection of new and replacement employees can ensure that new recruits are aligned with the organization's values and motivated to carry forward the corporate culture as part of their day-to-day activities. Regular communication of the culture and its values by the management team, combined with appropriate recognition and reward for employees who enthusiastically support the organization's values, will ensure that the delivery of good customer service is maintained as a critical part of the organization's business, regardless of staffing or other changes that the business faces in the future.

SERVICE ASSESSMENT

1. Take a close look at your company's culture. What five adjectives describe it best? What are the guiding values that govern employee behavior? Is this the way you want your organization to be perceived? If not, what will you do to change it?
2. What type of training is used to reinforce the company culture?
3. Who are the culture supporters of your company?

Glossary

audio newsletters—General information delivered via an auditory medium.

behavioral interviewing—A technique to determine candidate qualifications for a position in which the interviewer asks the candidate to provide specific examples of past behavior or experience as an indicator of potential success.

benchmark—A reference point for comparison.

buyer's remorse—The idea that any doubts the customer had before a purchase tend to be amplified after the purchase commitment has been made. Also known as post-purchase dissonance.

casual interviewing—A form of research which takes place through informal conversation.

CD-ROM based learning—Self-paced training, which takes place using an optical disk system and microcomputers.

communication—The process by which ideas or messages are exchanged between places or people.

communication barriers—Any obstacle, obstruction, or interference with a message being received and understood.

communication hierarchy—The flow of messages and information characterized by a group, persons, or things, arranged in successive orders.

communication paths—The directional flow of messages between groups or persons.

Communication Richness Scale—The relative value and effectiveness of the different types of communication methods widely used.

competence—The degree to which an individual possesses the technical and interpersonal skills to do a job.

consistency—Conforming to a set of principles that are in agreement with previous acts, statements, or decisions.

core values—The "golden rules" of operation that guide employee actions and words.

corporate culture—A system of common beliefs, values, and core principles that guide and dictate how people are to operate and behave in an organization.

corporate curriculum—All the programs and opportunities for learning afforded by an organization.

corporate culture—A system of common beliefs and values everyone who is part of an organization holds;

a set of core principles that guide and dictate the behaviors of those who play a role in delivering the company's products or services.

Critical Contact Points (CCP)—The steps of a service process where customers interact with representatives of the organization and form opinions based on the impressions received at each point in the process.

customer care—The process of understanding, communicating with, and supporting the needs of an organization's customers. Customer care includes the customer service function, but where traditional customer service has been primarily reactive after problems occur, the customer care function aims to be proactive in communicating with and managing information about customers to better understand and anticipate their needs before problems arise.

customer hotlines—Centralized telephone number through which customer telephone calls are filtered, making it easy for the customer to contact the manufacturer or service provider.

Customer Relationship Management (CRM)—An industry term for methodologies, technology, and capabilities that help an organization manage customer relationships in an organized and efficient manner Although often attributed to software applications that may form the core of a CRM initiative, the objective of CRM is to provide workers with the information and processes necessary to know their customers, understand their needs, communicate effectively with, and build stronger relationships between the company, its customer base, and its service partners.

Customer's "Bill of Rights"—A list of generally accepted requirements that represent the minimal needs and expectations for any service experience.

data mining—A process for analyzing records and databases to identify relationships between customer contacts, historical sales data, and customer service logs.

database—A group of related files organized to appear in one location so that they can be accessed and used in many different applications.

Decision Track—A diagram that represents all the steps followed for a process or service.

dissatisfaction—The state of being displeased or disappointed.

distance learning—Refers to a teaching method whereby students are geographically separated from the instructor or training facility, making use of the Internet, teleconference, or videoconferencing technology for progress monitoring and interaction

effective communication—Two-way dialogue between two or more people allowing for feedback between the parties to ensure that the message is properly received and understood.

electronic mail—The computer-to-computer exchange of messages and information.

emotional response—A reaction to a situation, which is based on a strong feeling, such as love, hate, or joy.

empowerment—Putting employees in charge of what they do.

expectation—The anticipation of an event as certain or probable.

explicit information—The literal words used to convey a message.

external communication—Messages which are transmitted to the general public outside of an organization and its employees, such as customers, the press, and governmental regulatory agencies.

extrinsic motivation—The willingness to exert high levels of effort toward organizational goals because of the potential for gaining a tangible reward.

focus group—A somewhat informal research group consisting of 6 to 10 people who are current or likely users of your product or service. They may be existing customers, interested parties, or completely anonymous groups selected by some predetermined criteria with specific objectives in mind. These people are invited to gather for a few hours to discuss a specific topic. A trained facilitator questions group members about their feelings and behavior toward your service delivery, and encourages as much free-flowing discussion as possible. The comments are recorded, and the answers provide a basis for more formalized survey construction.

formal communication—Communication networks that follow the authority chain and are usually limited to task-related items; includes the stated policies and procedures used to convey information about company activities, projects, and processes.

formal customized research—Data, which has been collected for a specific purpose and organization.

goal—A desired result towards which everyone is working.

good customer service—Service that exceeds expectations leaving customers very highly satisfied with the service and the product.

guiding principles—That part of the culture which forms a structural framework dictating how individuals will behave.

horizontal communication—The flow of information or messages from one peer group to another.

implicit information—The implied, but not expressly conveyed, message that transfers through such things as body language, tone of voice, or gestures.

industry research—Data which has been collected and refers to a specific branch or sector of business.

informal communication—Less structured information transfer that is free to move in any direction and skip authority levels, and includes what is known as the office grapevine.

integrity—The degree of honesty and truthfulness displayed by an individual.

internal communication—All information transfer that takes place inside an organization, between management, its employees, vendors, trade contractors, and customers, in the transaction of normal business activities.

Internet—A vast interconnected network linking business, governmental, scientific, and educational organizations and individuals around the world.

Intranet—An internal private network based on Internet technology.

intrinsic motivation—The willingness to exert high levels of effort toward organizational goals because it satisfies an inherent need from within, such as sense of achievement, responsibility, or competence.

job description—A written summary of the task requirements for a job and the personal characteristics necessary to do the tasks.

latency—The dormant period between initial purchase and the time a service request is made.

loyalty—The state of maintaining faith and confidence in any relation or obligation.

Mission Statement—A one-sentence explanation of everything the company stands for and describes what the company wants to be.

motivation—The willingness to exert high levels of effort toward organizational goals, conditioned by the effort's ability to satisfy some individual need.

National-Do-Not Call list—A registry enacted by the Do Not Call Act of 2003, which allows consumers to have their names placed on a national list, which prohibits telemarketers from contacting them.

natural complainers—This type of personality, depicted by complaints about some aspect of the service experience regardless of the relative quality of the service delivered, may be very demanding and especially difficult to satisfy.

needs—An urgent or essential requirement.

observational research—A type of research conducted by watching intently the actions and reactions of the targeted group without them knowing they are being observed.

openness—The degree of willingness to share information freely and willingly.

panel discussions—A discussion before an audience of a specific topic by a group of selected speakers.

performance standards—Criteria that specify how well, not simply how, work is to be done by defining levels of acceptable or unacceptable employee behavior.

point-of-service feedback—A system that captures information regarding the service experience at the time service is rendered.

post-purchase dissonance—The idea that any doubts the customer had before a purchase tend to be amplified after the purchase commitment has been made. Also known as buyer's remorse.

Problem Awareness Scale—A diagram that identifies the percentage of customer issues known by the different work groups in an organization.

published sources—Data and research that already exists, having been collected for another purpose.

rational response—A reaction to a situation that is based on reasoning.

realistic job preview—An overview of a position that includes the positive and unpleasant aspects of the job.

recognition—To demonstrate appreciation or approval of.

service barriers—Obstacles standing in the way of service delivery.

Service Delivery Zones—A diagram that shows the results that can be derived from a customer experience based on how well the customer's needs and expectations were met.

service goals—A desired result towards which everyone is working with respect to the delivery of customer service.

service mentors—A teacher, advisor, or sponsor who symbolizes the organization's service standards and can teach others how to model that behavior.

service standards—The pre-defined outcomes and accomplishments from the service effort that achieves customer expectations.

service partner—One who shares in part of the delivery process.

service-performance gap—The difference between service specifications and actual service satisfaction level.

Service Synergy Model—A graphic representation that provides the framework for departments to work together cooperatively and united in their actions towards the customers.

silo effect—A dysfunctional state that occurs when individual groups or departments are focused on their own narrow responsibility areas to the exclusion of the needs of other departments or the overall organization.

spam—Unsolicited bulk e-mails.

subject matter expert—One who has skill or knowledge in a functional area of an organization.

trade association research—Data that has been collected on behalf of a specific body of persons who have a common purpose.

trust—A characteristic of high-performing organizations where individuals believe in the integrity, character, and ability of each other.

vertical communication—The flow of information or messages from management to staff or staff to management based on levels of authority and responsibility.

video teleconference—The use of telecommunications technology to enable people to meet electronically and see each other on video screens.

vision—A realistic, credible, and attractive picture of the future for an organization or organizational unit that grows out of and improves upon the present.

web-based research and data collection—Information that is gathered using the Internet.

website—A place on the Internet where a company stores information about itself so that others may access and view it from their computers.

References

CHAPTER 1

1. Naisbitt, John. *Megatrends* (New York: Warner Books, Inc. 1982).
2. Peters, Thomas J. and Waterman, Robert H., Jr. *In Search of Excellence* (New York: Harper & Row Publishers. 982).
3. Incoming Calls Management Institute, "Industry Statistics" [data and commentary online]; available from ICMI website http://www.incoming.com.
4. FileNet Corporation 2002 Annual Report (Costa Mesa, CA).
5. Ibid., Incoming Calls Management Institute.
6. American Consumer Satisfaction Index, Quarter 4, 2002 [data and commentary online]; available from ACSI website http://www.acsi.com.
7. Festinger, L.A. A Theory of Cognitive Dissonance (Stanford, CA: Stanford University Press, 1957). Term in general usage derived from Festinger's original work.
8. Goodman, John, O'Brien, Pat, and Segal, Eden. Selling Quality to the CFO (TARP White Paper, March 2000).
9. "A Stock Theory Linking Price with Satisfaction Isn't Perfect," *The Wall Street Journal*, February 19, 2003.
10. Goodman, John, O'Brien, Pat, and Segal, Eden. *Selling Quality to the CFO* (TARP White Paper, March 2000).
11. Mirman, Robert. "5 Steps to Create a Customer Service Legend," *Southern California Builder Magazine*, August 1991.
12. Goodman, John. *Basic Facts on Customer Complaint Behavior and the Impact of Service on the Bottom Line* (TARP White Paper, June 1999).
13. Ibid.
14. Whitely, Richard C. *The Customer-Driven Company* (Reading, MA: Addison-Wesley Publishing Company, Inc., 1991).
15. Mirman, Robert. "Looking for the Answer to Sales and Survival," *Sun Coast Architect Builder Magazine,* June 1995.

CHAPTER 2

1. Covey, Stephen R. *The 7 Habits of Highly Effective People* (New York: Simon & Schuster, 1989).

CHAPTER 4

1. Berry, Leonard L., Bennett, David R., and Brown, Carter W.,*Service Quality: A Profit Strategy for Financial Institutions* (Homewood, IL: Dow Jones-Irwin, 1989), p. 39.
2. Goodman, John. "Basic Facts on Customer Complaint Behavior and the Impact of Service on the Bottom Line," *Competitive Advantage*, June 1999, pp. 1-5.
3. Fonvielle, William. "How to Know What Customers Really Want," *Training & Development*, September 1977, pp. 40-45.
4. Griffith, Joe. *Speaker's Library of Business Stories, Anecdotes and Humor* (Englewood Cliffs, NJ: Prentice Hall), p. 307.

CHAPTER 5

1. Robbins, Stephen P. *Organizational Behavior* (Saddle River, NJ: Prentice-Hall), pp. 180-181.
2. Parasuraman, V.A., Zeithaml, L.L., and Berry, "SERVQUAL: A Multiple-Item Scale for Measuring Consumer Perceptions of Service Quality," *Journal of Retailing,* Vol. 64, No. 1, p. 23.
3. Mirman, Robert. "Forget About Satisfying Your Customers," *Builder Digest of Northern California.*
4. Ibid., "Freud, Phobias and Referrals," *Builders Digest of Northern California.*
5. Ibid., "The Impact of Construction Quality on Referrals (Part 1 of a 2-Part Series)," *Builders Digest of Northern California.*

CHAPTER 6

1. Burger, Chester. *Survival in the Executive Jungle* (New York: MacMillan Publishing Company, 1964).
2. *Funk & Wagnall's Standard College Dictionary* (New York: Harcourt, Brace & World, Inc., 1966).
3. Yoshida, Sidney. "Quality Improvement and TQC Management at Calsonic in Japan and Overseas" (paper prepared for the Second International Quality Symposium in Mexico, November 1989).
4. Whitely, Richard. *The Customer Driven Company* (Reading, MA: The Forum Corporation, 1991).
5. "Communication without Words," *Psychology Today*, 1968.
6. Campbell, James, and Hepner, Hall, ed. "Nonverbal Communication: Exploration into Time, Space, Action, and Object," *Dimensions in Communication* (Belmont, CA: Wadsworth, 1970).

7. Kreitner, Robert. *Management, 6th Edition* (Geneva, IL: Houghton Mifflin Company, 1995).
8. Pike, Robert W. *Creative Training Techniques Handbook* (Minneapolis, MN: Lakewood Books, 1989).
9. Lemos, Robert. "Spam Hits 36 Percent of E-Mail Traffic," [online]; available from CNET News.com, August 29, 2002.
10. "Call Center Industry Statistics Related to COSTS/BUDGET," [online]; available from incoming.com, http://www.incoming.com/industryfacts/costs-budget.html, September 2003. First appeared in *Asia Pacific Call Centre News*, May 1, 2002.
11. Mirman, Robert. "Mel Gibson, Bad Golfers & Good Builders," *Builder and Developer,* Vol.7, No. 8.
12. Ibid., "Back to Basics: 10 Ways to Increase Sales," *Southern California Builder.*
13. Ibid., "Ultimate Advocate: The Sales Experience," *Big Builder Magazine*, June 2003.

CHAPTER 7

1. Belasco, James A., and Stayer, Ralph C. *Flight of the Buffalo* (New York: Warner Books, 1993).
2. Block, Peter. *The Empowered Manager.* (Indianapolis, IN: Jossey-Bass, 1991)
3. *Work Expectations Profile Research Report* (Wayzata, MN: Inscape Publishing, Inc., 2001).
4. Goodman, John. "Basic Facts on Customer Complaint Behavior and the Impact of Service on the Bottom Line," first published in *Competitive Advantage*, June 1999.
5. Schindler, P.L., and Thomas, C.C. "The Structure of Interpersonal Trust in the Workplace," *Psychological Reports*, October 1993.
6. Goodman, John. "Basic Facts on Customer Complaint Behavior and the Impact of Service on the Bottom Line," first published in *Competitive Advantage*, June 1999.
7. Mirman, Robert. "What Do the Best Builders Do Differently?" *Builder Marketing,* Vol. 6, No. 2.
8. Ibid., "One Year Later: The Homeowner's Perspective," *BIG BUILDER Magazine,* June 2003.

CHAPTER 8

1. Deal, Terrence E., and Kennedy, Allan A. *Corporate Cultures: The Rites and Rituals of Corporate Life* (Reading, MA: Addison-Wesley Publishing Company, 1982).
2. Kipnis, D. *The Powerholders* (Chicago: University of Chicago Press, 1976).
3. Cathcart, Jim. *Relationship Selling: The Key to Getting and Keeping Customers* (New York: The Putnam Publishing Group, 1990).

4. Deams, Richard. *Interviewing: More Than a Gut Feeling* (Urbandale, IA: American Media Publishing, 1998).
5. "New Survey Finds Companies Losing Best Candidates in Tight Labor Market, Poor Communications to Blame," *Business Wire*, January 27, 1998.
6. Kline, Peter, and Saunders, Bernard. *Ten Steps to a Learning Organization* (Arlington, Virginia: Great Ocean Publishers, 1993).
7. "Serving the American Public: Best Practices in Resolving Customer Complaints," Federal Benchmarking Consortium Study Report as reported in the *National Performance Review*, March 1996.
8. McMurrer, Daniel P., Van Buren, Mark E., and Woodwell, William H., Jr. *The 2000 State of the Industry Report* (Alexandria, VA: American Society for Training and Development, 2000).
9. Meister, Jeanne. *Corporate Quality Universities* (Burr Ridge, IL: Richard D. Irwin, Inc., 1994).
10. Broad, Mary L., and Newstrom, John W. *Transfer of Training* (Reading, MA: Addison-Wesley Publishing Company, 1992).
11. Newstrom, John W. "Leveraging Management Development through the Management of Transfer," *Journal of Management Development*, No. 5 (1986), 33-45.

Table pg 11 —
Pg 13 - Bott P
pg 14 prioritizing
pg 16 - (service not an afterthought.